To Love Again

Remarriage for the Christian

Helen Kooiman Hosier

ABINGDON PRESS

NASHVILLE

To Love Again: Remarriage for the Christian

Copyright © 1985 by Abingdon Press

Library of Congress Cataloging in Publication Data

HOSIER, HELEN KOOIMAN.
  To love again.
  Bibliography: p.
  1. Divorce—Religious aspects—Christianity. 2. Remarriage—Religious
aspects—Christianity. I. Title.
BT707.H67   1985   261.8'3589   85-15012
                  ISBN 0-687-42187-X
                  (pbk.: alk. paper)

Scripture quotations noted NASB are from the New American Standard
Bible, © The Lockman Foundation, 1960, 1962, 1963, 1968, 1971, 1973,
1975, 1977. Quotations noted TLB are from *The Living Bible*, copyright ©
1971 by Tyndale House Publishers, Wheaton, Ill. Used by permission.
Quotations noted NIV are from the Holy Bible: New International Version.
Copyright © 1978 by the New York International Bible Society. Used by
permission of Zondervan Bible Publishers. Quotations noted RSV are from
the Revised Standard Version of the Bible, copyrighted 1946, 1952, © 1971,
1973 by the Division of Christian Education of the National Council of
Churches of Christ in the U.S.A., and are used by permission. Quotations
noted KJV are from the King James Version of the Bible. Quotations noted AV
are from the Authorized Version.

MANUFACTURED BY THE PARTHENON PRESS AT
NASHVILLE, TENNESSEE, UNITED STATES OF AMERICA

—————— To ——————

those who have experienced the trauma of divorce and who have tried very hard, with God's help, to hold their marriages together—and to those who have gone on to remarry, agonizing over whether this was scripturally right. And to those Christians who understand that God's grace is big enough to cover the divorced and remarried. And to pastors who preach and practice compassionate theology, upholding the truth—the whole counsel of God—while extending love and going beyond forgiveness to demonstrate redemptive grace.

"Let us therefore come boldly unto the throne of grace, that we may obtain mercy, and find grace to help in time of need" (Heb. 4:16 KJV).

—————*Acknowledgments* —————

I am deeply grateful to the many divorced-remarried people who responded to my questionnaire, to others whom I interviewed personally, and to all who shared experiences and views in some way. In order not to reveal their identities, all names have been changed.

Because I am an avid reader, many thoughts and ideas I have read become so lodged in my thinking that they become a part of me. I realize, therefore, that many of my thoughts may have been expressed originally by someone else, either in writing or speaking. I am indebted to those who have contributed to my fund of knowledge through the years but to whom I could never give proper acknowledgment simply because their thoughts are now part of my own experience and thinking. For others, however, whom I have mentioned, and from whose books I have quoted, I owe a debt of gratitude for helping me so very much in shaping my thoughts and encouraging me. For others who encouraged me, who prayed for me, and did thoughtful things, thank you. Thanks also to Ray S. Anderson, Associate Dean, Fuller Theological Seminary, and Dennis B. Guernsey, for permission to use material from their book; and to Dr. Anderson, esteemed theologian, whose insights years ago provided courage and help, and with whom I have corresponded, special thanks for writing the foreword to this book.

Contents

Foreword

Divorce and remarriage is an issue that torments pastors, strains the ingenuity of biblical scholars, and plunges Christians into sickening and devastating shock. Over the past eight years, I have discussed this issue with more than eight hundred pastors enrolled in Doctor of Ministry studies, using a case study approach. These pastors are men and women trained in biblical exegesis and interpretation. The only consensus is that there is an uneasy conscience in the church over this issue and an agonizing uncertainty as to how Jesus' teaching and Jesus' healing can be received where it really counts—in the lives of men and women who look to God for guidance and help.

Is divorce and remarriage included in the gospel of Christ? Helen Hosier thinks so—and so do I.

Biblical scholars will continue to contend for competing interpretations of key New Testament texts, which speak to the issue of divorce and remarriage. This book does not attempt to resolve these attempts into a conclusive position. What we have in this book, instead, is what one might call a "hermeneutic of healing." Or, to put it another way, we are presented with an interpretation of God's ministry to the divorced person from the standpoint of one who experiences God's healing and restoration through this tragedy.

By sharing her own story and testifying to God's grace of healing, Helen Hosier calls to mind the perspective of the blind man who was healed by Jesus and whose theological reflection began with the confession, "One thing I know, that though I was blind, now I see" (John 9:25 RSV). There is an interpretation of the character and purpose of God that must also be heard from the living texts of those who have experienced the truth of his healing ministry.

There are responsible Christians who are rightly concerned for the biblical teaching about marriage and divorce. But there must also be concern for the biblical teaching about the character and nature of God as evidenced in his gracious work of healing and restoration of those who have become casualties of broken marriages.

For those of us who hold that Jesus was himself the "grace and truth" of God incarnate, his actions are as revelatory and authoritative as his words. This cannot be limited to the actions of Jesus as recorded in the gospels by which he consistently became the advocate of those who sought healing and restoration from their sins. The actions of Jesus today through the power of his Spirit help us to understand more fully the Word of Jesus in Scripture concerning marriage as a word of promise and hope, not a "written code [which] kills" (II Cor. 3:6 RSV).

I am happy to commend this book to all who are struggling with the issues of divorce and remarriage. Biblical scholars ought to listen carefully to its witness to the power of God both to kill and make alive, before concluding that Jesus, by his teaching, meant to establish a law of marriage apart from the freedom and power of God. Christians who view marriage as a contract that can be broken conveniently and painlessly need to read this book for the purpose of renewing the covenant of marriage at all costs through the healing grace of God-empowered love.

Those who are still caught in the sick undertow of divorce and those who are stranded on the beach, where the tide has gone out—carrying with it the dreams and hopes of love gone awry—need to follow the pilgrimage in this book to a new shoreline of love from God, which promises "all things new." And, finally, for those who are prepared to love and marry again, this book offers wise and wonderful counsel—these are the practical and sensible things that love cannot afford to leave to the unromantic and the unblessed. When Jesus blesses the marriage with his presence, the wine at the end is the best.

Ray S. Anderson
Associate Professor of
Theology and Ministry
Fuller Theological Seminary

Preface

Strong and healthy second marriages are raising many perplexing questions for the church today. On the one hand are those who insist that there will be devastating consequences if people divorce and remarry—consequences in the here and now, and for all eternity. On the other hand is the evidence of the marriages themselves. As we look at those whose first marriages were never marked by happiness and peace, but who now are partners in new marriages with spiritual growth, mutual happiness, and peace, it is obvious that something good is operating in these remarriages.

This is a book for those who have gone through divorce and are remarried; it is also for those who are divorced, alone, and hopeful about the future. And it is especially addressed to pastors, church leaders, and church members who do not understand how anyone could get a divorce when one of the commonly accepted "biblical reasons" for divorce did not exist. It is also for those who do understand God's redemptive grace as it relates to the divorced and divorced-remarried, and who seek ways to help others gain an understanding of how this is to be extended to others. *To Love Again* is a call to all Christians for understanding, grace, and an accepting of God's forgiveness, and then moving on—beyond forgiveness—to be an active part of the body of Christ, through the church—ministering help, healing, and hope to others who have been wounded.

To those who remain divorced and unmarried at the present time, I pray that within these pages you will discover some help and hope. That there will be new insights for you. Are you wondering if there is some kind of road map that will lead you to a new romance and remarriage? If there is one thing I have learned, it is the certainty that only when we are prepared *not* to marry again are we actually in a position where we can reconsider remarriage—that we can commit ourselves to a new marriage only when we are free not to. Ponder this paradox. The option of remaining single must always be realized as a legitimate alternative—certainly one that the apostle Paul writing under the inspiration of the Holy Spirit advised. But more on that in the book itself.

We do need to recognize that many second marriages end in divorce, too. Let us not deceive ourselves into thinking that a second marriage is easy, that we don't have problems in second marriages.

Some divorced Christians, and some divorced-remarried Christians have told me that the attitude of the church so at first unsettled them that they forfeited formal religion and worship in favor of a more personal relationship with God. Later, after the initial turbulence settled, they were once again able to walk back into church life. For many of these, this meant walking into a different church, fellowshiping with other believers, leaving their old lives behind, and walking on—out of bondage—into the liberty of Christ's love and mercy.

Whatever your experience, whoever you are—still married to your first love, whether happily or unhappily, or divorced, or divorced-remarried—I pray that you are showing forth God's mercy, forgiveness, understanding, compassion, and grace, for isn't that what He has asked us to do?

Helen Kooiman Hosier
Sunnyvale, California
November 1985

Divorce, Remarriage, and the Church

Chapter One

LEGALISM
Loveless Niceness in the Church

"Remarriage is out under any circumstances, including adultery. Dating for the divorced individual is also not an option."

I looked at the person sitting opposite me. Had I heard correctly? Later, he told me my face registered unbelieving shock. The words tumbled out. "Would you mind repeating that? I mean, I'm not certain I really heard you say what I think you said. Once more please, if you don't mind." And so my friend ran it by me again.

First he supplied the name of a well-known Christian organization. Then he stated, "They've taken a no-remarriage-under-any-circumstances stance, including adultery, and divorced individuals are not even to do any dating."

I had heard correctly, and I was stunned.

He continued, "Every week I have to deal with the casualties of that kind of rigid legalism. And interestingly enough, I find people *want* black and white answers until . . . " he paused, moving forward in his chair, *"until it is themselves or one of their children. Then they want to reap a harvest of compassion and understanding."*

I think like a writer. Long years of spending hours at the typewriter have developed a sense of visualizing a verbal statement in black and white print. That day I visualized those words in bold caps underlined. My mind staggered at the impact of what he was sharing. But I shouldn't have been so shocked; it wasn't the first time I had encountered this kind of view. In fact, my experience since my own divorce in February 1971, and my subsequent remarriage three years later, had been one encounter after another with the unfortunate victims of the tragedy of divorce. Futhermore, just about everything I read written from the Christian vantage point spoke against divorce and remarriage. It was difficult to find someone who believed God's grace was big enough to cover divorced people. It appeared that in one way or another, pastors, church leaders, writers, and Christians in general were making it difficult for divorced people to forget their status. As Dwight Hervey Small says, "Strange, but one can be forgiven nearly any other failure known to life and be restored to a place of service within the church—confession and penitence does the trick. But to be divorced and remarried is to have committed the unpardonable sin for which there is no restoration to service for Christ in the Church. This book [his book, *The Right to Remarry*] is a protest to all that, a call for an end to this kind of injustice and ecclesiastical immorality!"[1]

I find myself rushing to the side of those who have been divorced also—rushing in protest to things that are said about them, or things that are implied. Sometimes those whose marriages ended in divorce had survived a good many major crises, only to have their marriages explode into nothingness years later. Regardless of its duration, a shattered marriage leaves mangled memories and lots of pain. Pain, guilt, and problems of every size and description—often compounded by financial woes, and a lot of unforeseen agonies, not the least of which is the attitude of other Christians and some forms of social ostracism within the church. But gradually hope begins to emerge for the divorce victims. Others who have divorced have reconstructed their lives. They've been meeting some of these divorced-remarried people. They begin to think in terms of "I can, too." But just about the time hope is ready to burst into full bloom comes the devastating recognition that there is something else to consider. And it's a *major* consideration when you are a divorced Christian. What will the church say about remarriage?

When you are seeking to walk close to the Lord, wanting to be obedient to Him, even though you feel you've messed up your life quite badly with a failed marriage, another question hovers in the back of your mind: What does the Bible have to say about remarriage?

These are questions we don't like to confront. They are too painful. We are so busy trying to reconstruct our lives that it takes all of our emotional energy just to cope. We don't need more unanswered questions making an unwelcome incursion into the already overcrowded traffic patterns in our thinking. Also, we really aren't ready to entertain serious thoughts of eventual remarriage (let alone dating) in those first traumatic months of getting readjusted to life as singles.

But *when* we do—sometimes it's a few months later, for others it's much later—those questions *have* to be confronted. If you are a serious-minded Christian, you can't run away from them forever. How do you handle the questions?

A ton of books has been written in the last ten or more years on the subjects of divorce and remarriage. However, when I went through my divorce, not much had yet been written on the subject so I wrote *The Other Side of Divorce*. Writing the book was a struggle. I didn't want to hurt my former husband, his family, and our children. Neither did I want to write anything that would encourage divorce or provide a convenient out or escape for those contemplating divorce. I certainly didn't want to say anything that might be misconstrued as being vindictive, or that would be misinterpreted as bitterness; neither did I want to be accused of being defensive. Last, but certainly not least, I didn't want to bring reproach upon Christianity and the name of Christ.

The book was written and, I feel, God took care of every one of those things. Because He knew my heart, and He knew my love for Him and for others, I trusted Him to help me say what I felt needed to be said in a spirit of love.

Then came the day, however, when my friend sat opposite me sharing some stories of the casualties of rigid legalism that he, as a professional counselor, was encountering. "Helen, you need to address yourself now to the subject of remarriage."

21

I looked at him and quickly responded, "No way!"

"Don't be so sure," he said just as quickly. "Haven't people been helped by your book on divorce?"

I had to admit that the stacks of letters I'd received through the years, and the many encounters with individuals who talked about the impact that book had had on their lives, had been an encouragement to me.

"Do you think books on the subject of divorce have encouraged people—Christian individuals in particular—to seek divorce as an out from a marriage that wasn't too great?" he asked.

Of course there is no way anyone who has written on that subject can know the answer to that question, but my own experience in relating to others had shown me that my book had met a need, and it had made people pause and rethink their own situations. I also knew couples who had been able to reconstruct their marriages after reading the book—not many, but some had let me know this had happened.

"How do you feel about remarriage?" my counselor-friend asked me that day. "I know you have a good second marriage. How did you answer your own questions about what the church would say—other Christians—and certainly what the Bible says about the subject? How did you resolve that? Or didn't you?"

I had resolved it. I had confronted the questions. I had also talked about the subject of remarriage with other divorced-remarried individuals on numerous occasions.

Shortly after that discussion with my friend, I was confronted with an article on remarriage in one of our better-known Christian magazines, written by a divorced man I knew. He told me the article would be appearing, and he knew I'd be interested in reading it. Indeed I was anxious to see it, knowing his views as I did.

I had nothing but the greatest compassion for this man. His wife had left him. They were both Christians. Each time I had met him I sensed he was harboring a certain amount of bitterness in his heart.

I read the article. Toward the end, this man briefly made

reference to compassion and God's character of forgiveness toward those who repent. Quickly a question raced across my mind: Had he finally put his finger on the key that would help him unlock his own stored-up grievances?

A few minutes later I put the article down, my spirits sagging. His reasoning revealed that he felt genuine repentance required a willingness to forgive each other in a tangled marital situation and then to become reconciled.

Forgiveness. Reconciliation.

I couldn't have agreed more with his reasoning up to a point. But there has to be a willingness on the part of *both* to forgive, to work on the relationship, and to be reconciled. This is definitely the biblical ideal.

But what of forgiveness on the part of the one who feels the other party isn't holding out forgiveness? In this instance, he felt his wife, who left him, was unforgiving. (She did eventually remarry.) Who was withholding forgiveness? Had he really forgiven her for her contribution to the marital problems? Had he recognized his contribution to the failure of their marriage?

Reconciliation. What about peace? What if reconciliation attempts have ended in repeated disappointment, heartache, and unpeace?

Did I hear someone say, "Now you are talking about hardness of heart"?

Yes. The Bible certainly makes it plain that this happens. Cold, hardened hearts. Rotten relationships. Marriage in name only. But whose heart was cold? Which heart was hard—the man's or the woman's? Or was either of their hearts cold? I'm not so sure. Does the church (do Christians on the outside of these difficult situations) really have all the facts so that they can judge the condition of another's heart? The irreversible reality of marital breakup has hit the church full force; she turns, embarrassed, uncertain about what to do in the face of disruption of the marital commitment among her people. Human weakness in all its frailty has reared its face. The church and her leaders would like to cling to their comfortable position—their "scriptural fixation"—that says divorce is the consequence of particular sin or hardness of heart on the part of the persons involved, quoting Jesus' words on divorce and the Old Testament prophet's words that God hates divorce (Mal. 2:16). But we are living in an age of grace. Dwight Small poses some important questions. "Was marriage made for man, or man for marriage? Is God bound to certain laws which render compassion and grace and release impossible? Is His grace nullified by His law? Or is His law sometimes nullified by His grace?"[2]

I searched in vain in the magazine article for an emphasis that showed me the compassionate heart of Jesus in sticky, difficult marital situations that have no easy, pat answers. The Bible shows us Jesus' compassion as well as God's law. Dwight Small says, "His law can be rendered inoperable in a given situation by the action of His grace; it is not nullified, nor compromised in any way."[3] It is easy to concentrate on pointing out the law, and ignore God's mercy when we talk about divorce and remarriage. The man's article was rigidly legalistic.

What *did* Jesus do when confronted with heartbreakingly real situations? He neither turned His back on such individuals, nor did He add to their already burdened hearts. Small points out that in Christ's redemptive program, "mercy and grace supersede works-righteousness. Regardless of that which conditions God's will in the past or the future, Redemptive Realism governs His will for the present."[4]

It is true that the church and her people must continue to uphold the standards of righteous living set down for us in the Bible. To ask men and women who are committed to preaching and teaching the truth to do anything less is not right. But in the process we must reckon with the sin factor in relationships, which has resulted in divorce for some of us. By sin I mean a falling short of God's perfection. Some divorces, however, are the result of failure—not particular sin. These are marriages doomed almost from the outset for various reasons. Some of us then remarry. Others are contemplating doing so. Still others look forward to meeting the right person someday, hoping remarriage can take place.

Remarriage. Can Christians open their hearts with enough compassion to embrace the divorced-remarried Christians among them? When remarried Christians are excluded from the circle of love, the church may be every bit as guilty of lovelessness as it is convinced they have been in divorcing to begin with.

The man who wrote the magazine article sent me a statement a minister had written in response to the article, suggesting that all the clergy in America give the article a thirty-minute standing ovation. His note to me ended with a question, "Nice, huh?" followed by a smiley face and a question mark.

And that rather haunts me. It is *good* (I do not think *nice* is the right word) for the clergy in America to be convinced of the need to uphold biblical standards. It is not only good, but necessary. But for divorced-remarried Christians, or those contemplating remarriage, that kind of attitude quite often smacks of a loveless niceness. It comes across as so rigidly uncompromising as to be almost pharisaical—imposing guilt, hurt, more pain, and conflict. It opens wounds that may have begun to heal. Those caught in the crossfire would like fellow Christians to understand that we, too, have feelings, hopes, aspirations, *and* needs. And we have to ask, where is the biblical principle of liberating grace for those who are divorced or divorced and remarried? What do you do, for instance, with Hebrews 4:16, which says, "Let us therefore come boldly unto the throne of grace, that we may obtain mercy, and find grace to help in time of need." That theme is woven throughout the Epistles, and I do not read anywhere that it says to exclude the divorced.

Divorced individuals and divorced-remarried couples need the same recognition as sinners saved by the same grace that saved those who haven't failed as we have failed or committed that particular "sin."

Notes

1. Dwight Hervey Small, *The Right to Remarry* (Old Tappan, N.J.: Revell, 1975), p. 12.
2. Ibid., p. 21.
3. Ibid.
4. Ibid.

Chapter Two

People or Principle?

In any group of Christians, were the subjects of divorce and remarriage to come up, it is doubtful you could come to a consensus. In fact, you'd get a great many emotional responses. I think it is safe to say that the divorce-remarriage issue is the most sensitive pastoral and personal problem that the church and individual Christians face, a problem that incites more differences of opinion than almost any other problem the Christian world faces.

There are some who can accept divorce. It happens—even to some of the nicest people you know. So, let's get on with living. Others can't handle divorce at all—it's just not an option open to Christians.

Others say, "Oh yes, provided adultery was involved, then it's okay for the offended party to divorce." So one person gets off the hook.

But remarriage! Were the subject to be brought up among some Christians, opinions would explode all over the place.

You may be asking, "Are churches and Christian organizations really maintaining a 'no-remarriage' stance in *this* day and age?"

Underlying that question, which I have heard many times, is the assumption that since we are living in such an enlightened society, certainly enlightenment has spilled over into the church and religious organizations.

Let's think about that for a moment. There's another side to the coin. The Christian's enlightenment does not come from *Cosmopolitan* magazine! Of course we are living in what is called an enlightened society, but the Bible still has the right name for much of what we see going on all around us and about which we read in our magazines, books, and newspapers, and what we view on television. It's called *sin.* By any other word it's whitewashed. (And the Bible has something to say about whitewash, too!)

So divorced Christians, whether remarried or not, cannot measure their standards of right and wrong by the secular world's standards. To do so is to deceive ourselves. There is no hopscotching through the Bible, jumping over verse 9 of Matthew 19, for instance, to get into something more palatable.

Certainly not all churches and Christian organizations are legalistically rigid about divorce and remarriage. Many churches have a vital ministry for the divorced individuals in their community. Some churches relate beautifully to divorced people, attempting to help them in all sorts of ways, realistically walking with them through their problems and the emotional disarray in their lives. Too often, however, the help stops short when the individual finds someone to love and comes to the church pastor and the elders to talk about remarriage. At that point, the door of help slams shut, particularly when it is learned that the divorced person did not have one of the biblical reasons, in the first place, for getting a divorce. The verdict is no remarriage.

Consistently, in the available literature, you will find statements such as this:

I believe that the right of remarriage is always granted to someone whose divorce was permitted by God.[1]

God's Word clearly teaches that marriage is for life. Only upon the death of a spouse is one free to remarry. Divorce and remarriage while the first spouse yet lives constitutes adultery. For the divorced believer there are basically two options—reconciliation or the single life.[2]

> Scripture teaches that God's "divine concession to human weakness" is occasionally justified, allowing the Christian divorced person the right and freedom to remarry in the Lord. There are three such cases set forth in God's Word, each provided by His grace:
>
> First, when the marriage and divorce occurred prior to salvation (II Cor. 5:17).
>
> Second, when one's mate is guilty of sexual immorality and is unwilling to repent and live faithfully with the marriage partner (Matt. 19:9).
>
> Third, when one of the mates is an unbeliever and willfully and permanently deserts the believing partner (I Cor. 7:15).[3]

Many more such statements could be culled. These statements from clergymen represent the thinking and teaching of those who hold to a no-remarriage stance—unless it can be proven that they had one of the three reasons listed as their grounds for divorce.

This stance leaves out a vast number of Christian divorced individuals who (1) were Christians when they married (so the first justification for divorce would not apply); (2) did not leave their mate because he or she was involved in sexual immorality (so the second justification for divorce does not apply); and (3) their mate was not an unbeliever and did not desert him or her who was the believer (so the third justification for divorce does not apply).

So where does this stance leave us? Has the church considered what this does to us? How this makes us feel? This policy leaves us divorced, without the biblical reason to remarry. We can worship in the church as a single person—just not remarry.

Charles Swindoll says there is something much worse than living with a mate in disharmony. "It's living with God in disobedience."[4]

The other answer found in the literature is that there are dire consequences to be faced if remarriage takes place. We are told, for instance, that those who are not responsive to the scriptural options available for the divorced person need to be warned of the devastating consequences of remarriage. They point to Mark 10:1-12, Luke 16:18, and Proverbs 6:32-33, citing the severe consequences awaiting those who violate God's plan for marriage. Also, Hebrews 12:6-11 shows that God will discipline sinning Christians that they may share His holiness and yield the peaceful fruit of righteousness, and that such divine discipline is not a happy experience. Several biblical examples of this are given: II Samuel 12:9-13; II Samuel 13:1-10; II Samuel 15-18; Psalm 51—illustrations from the life of David.

In this same regard, I Corinthians, chapter 10, provides Old Testament examples of people who "lusted after evil," and who "set their hearts on evil things" (see v. 6 AV). Verse 11 of that chapter sums it up by stating, "Now these things happened to them as an example, and they were written for our instruction, upon whom the ends of the ages have come" (NASB).

Another answer set forth by Jay E. Adams, a theologian, frequent lecturer, and prolific writer on the topic of Christian counseling, lists fourteen steps the church must take to try and bring about a peaceful settlement of all the issues that arise in divorce cases among Christian couples.[5] The example used is a fairly typical situation—the individuals have gone their separate ways, he to another church while she remained in the church they had attended as a couple. The divorce had already taken place. According to this counselor, that was mistake number one, because the church kept a hands-off stance.

It is his feeling (and the expressed opinion of other theologians and writers on the subject) that the church should get involved *before* the divorce occurs. This is not only biblical but sometimes is the means whereby the couple can receive much needed help, and the marriage is salvaged and strengthened. To be sure, in many situations the couple don't want the church "interfering," but Matthew 18:15ff. speaks to the necessity of church discipline, and I Corinthians 6 discourages lawsuits between Christians. If couples will go this route—receiving the admonitions of the church, beginning counseling toward a new sort of life-style, and working towards a transformation in their marriage—fewer divorces among Christian couples would take place today. In many instances this *is* done, but even then, the attempts at restoration and reconciliation are not always successful. It is at this point where many counselors fail to show the mercy, and exercise the Christian graces so needed by both the man and woman in these complex and emotionally charged relationships.

Adams referred to the man he called Joe as leaving his church in "unrepentant anger," and when the pastor of Joe's church called him to see why, Joe "read him the riot act," demanding that the church send a letter of transfer to the church he was now attending. Joe stated that he had gotten the divorce because he was "tired of arguing and fighting about everything." Joe may very well have had legitimate reasons for feeling as he did. Incompatibility, however, is a nonbiblical ground for seeking divorce. But the strain of living a lie does finally take its toll and, in this case, Joe decided to end the deception. Churches that take the stance of no divorce without one of the commonly accepted biblical reasons cannot handle Joe's reason for divorce, yet this reason is being encountered in so many divorces among Christians. Neither commits adultery, but the continual repression of problems and an inability to live peaceably together results finally in an unwanted divorce. It's not that either the man or the woman is "stubbornly desisting" the church, God, or anyone else, it's just they've grown so far apart that not even marital counseling can help.[6]

Patti Roberts in her book, *Ashes to Gold*, describes her feelings about this with brave candor: "I am convinced that there comes a point in any unhappy marriage where there is so much accumulated bitterness and hurt and mutual distrust that, barring a miracle, it cannot be healed. Of course, God can and does work miracles, but we didn't have the faith or even the desire to receive one any more. Richard and I had both reached the point where we were no longer able to seek wholeness."[7]

Divorce then becomes the only option if such individuals are to retain a degree of emotional stability. This was my own situation. It wasn't that I wanted a divorce—else why would I have hung in there for twenty-three years? I hoped against hope—as so many do, I have since learned—believing, trusting, asking for a miracle, and doing everything possible to help bring such a miracle about. Can you begin to imagine how it hurts then to have fellow Christians look down their noses at you? You know they are falsely judging you, making disparaging remarks. It cuts to the quick. Tragically many Christians today are stoically enduring bad marriages just to avoid the embarrassment of getting a divorce, which would jeopardize their positions in the Christian world. They know friends would be forced to choose sides, and the alienation is something they don't want to face. It's not that they are so loyal to the Lord and His church—although that would be the case in some instances—but, more than likely, they want to hang onto all the good things that come with being a member in good standing of their local church. Some of these people are preachers or counselors themselves—highly respected, very visible men and women—and some of them are involved in ministries that are dependent upon the financial support of their followers.

Patti Roberts talks about that too, pointing out that some of these people (in difficult marriage situations) often feel owned by, and responsible to, the ministry even more than they feel reponsible to God. God forgives, but institutions do not. The institution—the ministry, the writing, the counseling, what-ever—demands loyalty. While God is patient, long-suffering, and gentle, institutions are not. And neither are the followers of institutions, nor the church members. "Institutions scream louder than God and it is human nature to respond to that which speaks loudest and most insistently. So, rather than risk angering the institution, some Christians continue to live fragmented, destructive lives. But holding a marriage together for the sake of the ministry rather than the sanctity of their scriptural vows does not please God. God places tremendous importance on truth in human relationships, and when two people are living a lie in order to protect a ministry, they are violating God's definition of marriage."[8]

31

The church is asking couples to endure bad relationships in the name of Christianity; yet the entire thrust of the New Testament is love. What is that stance but a farce? Playacting. Only it's not funny. It is tragic that so many married couples live in what I call a state of undivorce—married, but divorced from love and the reality of living together in a healthy, nourishing relationship. Not only they, but their children, suffer.

In Joe's case, it all came to a head when his ex-wife, Mary, came to her church and wanted to remarry. Her church took a strong stand against remarrying divorced persons under circumstances where the former spouse was still alive and unmarried. Dr. Adams explains that this is typical of many churches in which this strong stand actually grows from great weaknesses in the care and discipline of members.

Dr. Adams points out the many new complications that arose when Mary wanted to remarry: (1) Mary isn't free to remarry; (2) Joe has been deprived of his rights to church discipline; (3) Joe hasn't been confronted at all levels (according to the requirements of Matthew 18:15ff.) and is still considered a member of Christ's church in good standing despite his rejection of Christ's authority in the Bible; (4) a sinful divorce has been ignored; and (5) Joe (and Mary) stand in peril of commiting adultery.

Dr. Adams points out fourteen steps that he recommends "in order to clean up the many messes" that the church encounters in situations such as this. (1) The first church must seek God's forgiveness, forgiveness from Mary and Joe, and from the second church for failing to handle matters scripturally at the outset. (2) Mary must be advised to seek reconciliation following the procedures of Matthew 18:15ff., step by step. (3) Joe should be called upon to repent and seek reconciliation with Mary and his former church. (4) If all goes well, Mary and Joe will be reconciled, remarry, and build—under proper care and counseling—a new and better marriage. (5) If that doesn't work out, and "Joe sinfully refuses to be reconciled," (6) Mary should pursue Matthew 18:15ff, and (7) Joe's new church should be asked by Mary to become involved, since Joe should now be under its discipline. (8) Joe's new church should be aware of what has happened since Mary's congregation should have contacted them (according to step one). (9) If Joe's church "does what it should, well and good. Joe will repent or will be excommunicated, setting the matter to rest." (10) But what if Joe's church fails to "assume its responsibilities and will not excommunicate Joe, even though he fails to heed advice?" The answer provided is that this church is sinning, and this is going to further complicate matters. (11) At that point, the officers of Mary's church "must humbly confront the officers of Joe's church (it might begin with pastor confronting pastor, but if that fails, officers confronting officers) to try to resolve the matter, offering help, support, direction, encouragement, etc." (12) And it's really great if Joe's church agrees. "All will flow naturally to one of the two presented ends: reconciliation or discipline. But what if Joe's church refuses? Obviously, as it has all along, its sin further complicates matters." (13) At that point, Mary's church, has only one alternative left. Adams warns that this is to be used with "great caution when *every* effort has failed." They are "to declare (by a functional judgment) Joe's church to be as no church since it refuses to hear Christ's authority. . . ." But what about Joe? Oh, he is to be declared "as a heathen and a publican." (14) And Mary? What about Mary? "At long last, all threads have been pulled; the matter is set to rest, and on the basis of I Corinthians 7:15, Mary is eligible to marry another."[9]

That's an answer?

Well, admittedly it's been a bit messy along the way and hard on a lot of people involved, and possibly a lot of bitter words have been exchanged, and emotions have flared, but still, the institution has been preserved—and that's *very* important!

As I read Adams' material on Joe and Mary, several things leap off the page, arresting my attention, and I am disturbed by what is implied. First, Adams states that Joe has rejected Christ's authority in the Bible. I'm not so sure. Joe has spread out his hands and said, "God, I can't go on living a lie; I'm so tired of the fighting and arguing, and we're not getting any this marriage. I'm miserable; Mary is miserable. no companionship; no meeting of each other's deep eds. God, forgive me, but I see no other option." He's thi n himself on God's mercy. Is that rejecting Christ's authority?

Second, step number five says that if "Joe sinfully refuses to be reconciled," Mary should pursue Matthew 18:15ff. How can it be said that the man is "sinfully" refusing to be reconciled when he and Mary have lived together for years in a state of unpeace? What he's now done is to admit that they've been living a lie and since God sees his heart, he isn't fooling God (he may have fooled the church, her pastor, and her leaders), he wants to live openly and honestly before the world too.

Third, why is Mary getting off the hook so easy? It's Mary who wants to marry another man. How naive to assume that *she's* ready to be reconciled!

Fourth, why is it assumed that Joe hasn't repented, that he hasn't sought God's forgiveness (see point number 9)?

What the whole thing sounds like is a contrived effort to get Mary out of a situation where her church feels uncomfortable about letting her remarry and remain a member in good standing.

Granted, church discipline is a much neglected thing. I have long maintained that we, as a body of believers comprising the local church, do not deal well with "sin in the camp." We allow situations to fester and grow out of control. In this regard, I agree with Adams who also maintains this is a great weakness within the church. And in this regard, I read with particular interest Don Baker's book, *Beyond Forgiveness*, which deals with a real-life drama, showing the potential for restoration, transformation, and the possibility for revival in the church when steps are taken to properly administer discipline with love. Step by step, this pastor takes the reader through the incredibly heartbreaking account of how a staff member's sin was discovered, how he was confronted, and then how the church responded biblically to this fallen brother. In contrast to the Adams account, the primary purpose of the way this discipline was handled was to effect restoration—not retribution. (I admit that the circumstances in these accounts vary significantly, of course, which may account, in part, for the differences I see.) Joe had not sinned blatantly (the man in Baker's book had been unfaithful to his wife ten times). Neither, it seems to me, was Joe's new church sinning. I do not believe the situation with Joe and Mary (or any other divorced person who wishes to remarry) requires the entire church (or its leaders and pastor) to become embroiled in such controversy.

Is it any wonder so many Christian divorced people quietly slip away from the church? They would avoid that kind of mess. I've seen them sever relations with their friends of years' standing in order to move on to rebuild their lives, relying solely on their own relationship with God, trusting Him to look into their hearts and read motives based on His actual knowledge of all that has preceded the separation and divorce. I can now tell it—this is what I did.

In my own case, I knew the Bible passages; I knew the need for church discipline, rather than going to court and getting involved in legal proceedings. I had convinced my first husband to seek Christian counseling with me outside of our church. The fact that I finally instigated the divorce was *not* the fault of the Christian counselor (some may think—"He didn't do his job well"). No, it wasn't that at all. A supreme, all-out effort was made to save the marriage. But it would have been saving the *institution* of marriage only; there was no relationship left to salvage. At that point I called a halt to the pretense, thrust myself upon God's mercy, and I did as Joe did.

A Christian magazine invited pastors from various representative churches to write on the subject of "Marriage after Divorce?" and what the Scripture says about this. The introductory editorial comment stated: "Far more controversial than the subject of divorce is the subject of whether or not remarriage is permissible after divorce."

One of the representative ministers said: "The resolution of personal problems, when done at the expense of institutional principles, will bring only short-lived relief to filial and social ills."[10]

Amazing statement from that pastor! Can you call five, ten, twenty, or more years of a good solid second marriage "short-lived relief"? We all know people whose second marriage has lasted a *long* time. I know some of them who have had to keep the fact that they were divorced long ago a secret, but their marriage is looked upon as a shining example of what a good solid marriage should be. How shocked their churches would be if they only knew! I just wonder what has happened in that pastor's church in the last decade and a half, especially when the divorce rate among evangelical Christians has jumped right along with the divorce rate across the board in this country.

Another of those ministers, responding to the question of whether or not remarriage is permissible after divorce, wrote:

Basically, there are three views on this: (1) Remarriage is never justified; (2) Remarriage is justified only in certain prescribed circumstances: e.g., for the innocent party in adultery; (3) Remarriage is permitted not by man's righteousness or merit, but because of God's grace and mercy.

Turning to Scripture, you can find that some support can be gained for any of the three positions. On the one hand, you have the statement of Jesus: "Whoever marries a divorced woman commits adultery" (Matt. 5:32 RSV), and on the other hand you have the forgiveness and grace exemplified by Christ's statement to the woman taken in adultery: "Neither do I condemn thee: go, and sin no more" (John 8:12 KJV).

There are those who say that when there is evidence of adultery, before divorce, the innocent party can remarry without sin. But this is assuming that the "innocent" party is completely innocent. In any divorce, it is impossible to say that one is guilty and the other is innocent. It is only a matter of degrees of guilt.

Therefore, I believe that if remarriage privileges depend on the righteousness of one of the parties, then no remarriage is permissible.

However, I do not believe that this is the true spirit of Christ.

Because every broken marriage vow is a sin, I have no right as a minister of Christ to tell anyone—no matter how supposedly innocent they may appear—that they are justified in remarriage. But because Christ said, "Go and sin no more," to a prostitute, I do not believe that I have the right to deny the possibility of remarriage to anyone who truly is repentant and seeking God's mercy and grace.

To you, this may seem to be the easy way out. It isn't. Honestly bringing life under the judgment of the absolute ethic of Christ is always a painful thing. It either produces repentance and faith or self-justification and rebellion.

You may say, "This will encourage divorce and easy marriage." But I say that far more remarriages performed through the security of human righteousness ("innocent" party) are outside of the will of God than those remarriages that humbly acknowledge failure and sin and in repentance are seeking God's grace.

I fear that the Church often takes refuge in predetermined answers that leave the individual caught in failure without the grace of God. What right have we to place the burden of participating in the failures of humanity upon the head of the nearest Justice of the Peace who cannot possibly offer grace to meet the exigency of sin?

Let the Church be a channel of God's grace, refusing to place stigmas upon those who have sinned and been forgiven. If the Lord Himself is merciful and loving and forgiving, should His church be any less so?[11]

In the next chapter I'll tell you about Jim and Mitzi—a couple representative of many other Christian couples struggling with these rotten relationships. The question that Christians and the church are faced with is this: Do we put people over principle, or principle over people? Is the institution (the church, the institution of marriage) more important than the people in the institution?

Notes

1. David Hocking, *Marrying Again* (Old Tappan, N.J.: Fleming H. Revell Co., 1983), p. 28.

2. J. Carl Laney, *The Divorce Myth* (Minneapolis: Bethany House Publishers, 1981), p. 127. Academically and professionally, this is one of the best presentations drawing together what the Bible says on the subject of divorce and remarriage. I respect the author's views and recognize his own obvious compassion towards those who struggle with divorce and remarriage.

3. Charles R. Swindoll, *Divorce* (Portland, Ore.: Multnomah Press, 1981), pp. 20, 21. Chuck Swindoll is one of my favorite authors and favorite people. I respect him greatly. He says he wrote this little booklet on divorce "with *a sigh.*" A heavy heart was his companion as he forced himself to address this subject which he calls "a plague in our society that has reached epidemic proportions." I know the feeling. I, too, have done a lot of sighing with a heavy heart. As you will see throughout my book, I uphold every word of Scripture, but I have a big concept of the grace of God that I know reaches

to those of us who have experienced the breakup of our marriages. I know that to my loving, heavenly Father, marriage is ideally indissoluble. But throughout the Word, we do see that the divine ideal, though always perfect and correct, has a weak link—we are it. I have come to understand, therefore, that divorce may be a caring and redemptive way to end the falsehood of a marriage that was doomed to remain a sickly and distorted parody of what a Christian family should be.

4. Ibid., p. 22.

5. Jay E. Adams, *Marriage, Divorce, & Remarriage in the Bible* (Phillipsburg, N.J.: Presbyterian and Reformed Publishing Co., 1980). Dr. Adams makes a genuine effort to be fair in his exegesis of the Scriptures. I might also add that I sensed a desire to be compassionate towards the unfortunate victims of divorce. What I think he fails to understand, however, even though he repeatedly says that the problem is complex and emotionally charged, *is* how very, very difficult it is for those involved in marital misery to be reconciled. Adams urges that the church follow the path of "the reconciliation dynamic," i.e., following the principles of biblical reconcilia-tion. When such reconciliation does not take place, and the couple goes on to divorce, he (and so many others within the church) wrongly assume that one or the other of the principles involved—the man or the woman—rejected the help and authority of Christ and His church. Adams says, "By plugging in the reconciliation/discipline dynamic to the marriage-divorce-remarriage problem, the solution to 99 percent of these cases that heretofore may have seemed unsolvable immediately may be seen" (see p. 58 of his book).

He makes it seem so easy. It isn't! And the people who responded to my questionnaire were willing for reconciliation and, for the most part, didn't want a divorce to take place. These were good, solid, Bible-believing, church-attending Christians—many of them active in positions of leadership, some of them pastors.

In some respects, I felt Adams' book lacks an emphasis on God's grace, mercy, and forgiveness, although he does say there are many wrong attitudes in the conservative churches about divorce and divorcees. "From the way that some treat divorced persons, you would think that they had commited the unpardonable sin. Let us make it clear, then, that those who wrongfully (sinfully) obtain a divorce must not be excused for what they have done: it *is* sin. But precisely because it is sin, it is forgivable. The sin of divorcing one's mate on unbiblical grounds is bad, not only because of the misery it occasions, but especially because it is an offense against a holy God. But it is not so indelibly imprinted in the life of the sinner that it cannot be washed away by Christ's blood" (see p. 24). In these and other similar statements, Adams is calling for the church to exhibit forgiveness. "What I am urging is a proper (biblical) attitude on the part of God's church. To fail in this is serious; many lives (including the whole church) cannot escape the adverse effects—all will be hurt" (see p. 25).

What I see in Adams' book, and the efforts of other theologians writing on the subject, is a determined attempt to stand solid and firm on what they see the Bible saying on the subjects of divorce and remarriage. In doing so, it appears, at times, that there is little emphasis on God's grace. Unfortunately, Adams and others who have not been there—who have not gone through the trauma of a marriage relationship that was so sub-ideal—fail to recognize the severity of the problems divorced couples (or those contemplating divorce) have struggled with—many of them for decades! In this regard, some of these books come across in places as offering simplistic advice for *enormous* problems.

6. Adams, see p. 89.

7. Patti Roberts with Sherry Andrews, *Ashes to Gold* (Waco, Tex.: Word Books, 1983), p. 112.

8. Ibid., p. 113.

9. Paraphrased and summarized from Adams, p. 90. I don't believe it is necessary to point out to the reader all the complexities that arise as you look at the fourteen steps. It's all so cut and dried. But put yourself in Joe's shoes if you can. Because it was Mary's church (which was, at one time, also his church) that entered in and tried to effect a reconciliation (which failed), Mary got off scot-free and Joe was to be considered as an infidel. But what about Mary? Hadn't she contributed to the "arguing and fighting" that Joe said characterized their marriage? Yet at no point in the fourteen steps do you find Mary looking bad.

10. Oral Collins, "Marriage after Divorce?" *Eternity,* May 1966, p. 17.

11. Ray S. Anderson in the same article. Used by permission from the author. Pp. 16, 17.

Chapter Three

DIVORCE
The Pain and the Possibility

My husband Herman and I have lived in six different cities in three different states in the years since our marriage, and we've bumped into some complicated and unhappy marriage situations wherever we've gone. Some of the couples we have met are in the process of going through divorce, or, like us, they have been there and are now happily remarried. Still others were recently divorced—or not so recently—and are living as singles. All of these were Christian people, and we had no reason to doubt their relationships to the Lord were real.

My husband and I have also been with many married couples where the undercurrent of anger between the individuals was so strong you had the feeling you could almost reach out and touch it. These were people living a lie, putting on a respectable front. The hostile humor that flew between them at times was anything but funny; rather it was a subtle way of getting their digs in to the other. Very unpleasant, to say the least.

In order to gather material for this book, I sent out interview questions to divorced-remarried couples. A surprising number of the respondents related that they knew they were making a mistake on their wedding day, but they were committed to going through with the marriage and did not wish to embarrass their families, because they were all Christians and it was a church wedding. Besides that, they were young and hopeful, and the one who was having second thoughts—

usually the woman—didn't trust her emotions at the time of the wedding, and hoped her ambivalent feelings could be explained as the normal reaction of a nervous bride. Time proved her wrong, however, and she recognized she'd made a mistake. In spite of this, she worked on the marriage, had children, was a dutiful wife and mother, read books on how to improve the relationship, and attended seminars.

Male respondents admitted that they came into the marriage with a long list of things that they were going to change about their wives after the marriage. Women admitted this, too, but more men indicated that they felt this was a major source of trouble. "All I can say about such lists is that they should be junked, and these things should be talked out before marriage," one very candid gentleman wrote. "When you get married and then spring these lists (whether written or just in your head) on one another, even if done surreptitiously, it means there is an area of dishonesty, because between the making of those lists and enforcing those ideas, there was that promise to love, honor, and obey until death did you part." What I gathered from this and similar statements was the undisguised fact that both men and women entered into first-time marriages with unrealistic expectations that never materialized. The lines of communication were down before marriage, and they never got raised to a good level afterwards.

Young, idealistic, immature. These are words that surfaced in the questionnaires. Some of the respondents said they know they married for the wrong reasons the first time. It was the thing to do; all of their friends were either married or getting married. Some admitted to having to get married—they'd experimented sexually and pregnancy resulted. Others married to get away from home and out from under the thumb of what they felt were domineering parents.

In my own case, I married to get a father. I didn't recognize this at the time, of course, but I fell in love with my first husband's family and admired his father tremendously from the first Sunday we met. In order to understand this, you have to know that my father died a few months before I was born. My mother never remarried. I was starved for a father's love.

My first husband's parents are still my family. After my divorce, I didn't divorce myself from them, nor did they distance themselves from me. It took time for healing to take place, but we all worked at maintaining a relationship. My second husband has been accepted by them. We visit when we are in their part of the state; we exchange letters, telephone calls, and cards on special occasions. Even as I have written this, the morning mail brought a lovely card from my former mother-in-law, in which she sent a photo of my grandson (her great-grandson), and talked proudly of his school accomplishments. She thanked me for something I'd sent her, and the card was signed: Love as ever, Dad and Mother.

I know this isn't always the case and that the disruption of a marriage brings peculiar pain in the severance of relationships other than that with one's spouse. Would to God that this were not true, and we would practice the principles of forgiveness so plainly set forth in the Bible. So convinced was I of the need for this, that I worked to help bring it about in our family situation from the day I first decided on the divorce. If we could not work out our relationship in marriage, for the sake of our relationship with God, and with our children, grandchildren, and other family members, it was imperative that we forgive and forget. I can tell you that the possibility of living in peace with the person you were once married to does exist outside the marriage relationship itself. But it does take work. Questionnaire respondents indicated that many of them were still struggling with this. The bitterness and vindictiveness of former mates (and the human but sinful desire to seek revenge) surfaces easily. This is especially true when one or the other, or both of you, remarry.

Out of my own early struggle with the need to forgive came a book entitled *It Feels Good to Forgive.* In that book, I said that unless we have faced the need for unfaltering forgiveness, both of ourselves and extending it to others, one day we may discover that heaven is smaller than we think. My plea is that the reader will hasten to forgive. It truly does feel good. But far more important, God will honor this commitment. We need God's blessing and forgiveness on our lives whether we remain single or remarry. (For more on forgiveness, see chapter 6.)

Without exception, questionnaire respondents felt they had given the first marriage a chance—some for as long as twenty or more years. What they were saying is that they didn't give up easily; they had worked at it, and both felt they were Christians. It is disheartening to realize that too often the church just assumes that the couple *didn't* work hard enough at their marriage. The implication is that they didn't receive counseling, or the right counseling, or if they did, that they just went through the motions of pretending to be counseled so that later on, after the divorce, they could say they'd been counseled. That's generally not true—the couple involved, if they have any Christian commitment at all, don't just give up without expending a lot of effort to seek ways to make the marriage work. Usually they've talked to counselors, their pastor, friends. It's hard for outsiders to get involved. They don't want to take sides, especially if they've known the couple for years and have been friends. But in most instances, people will do what they can to help a couple get back together. Friends will serve as a sort of sounding board so the couple can bounce off their thoughts and feelings.

Herman and I have witnessed this several times, and we've been participants in this kind of counseling. When these discussions occur, we do not compromise the teachings of the Bible. There are no loopholes. We urge couples, if there is any shred of love left between them, to build on it. But we are not God; neither the church, nor anyone called upon to counsel will ultimately pronounce judgment on the lives and actions of Christians who have divorced and remarried. We do assure these individuals that God's compassion and understanding are greater than anything mere humans can offer when we come to Him sincerely repentant and ask His forgiveness and help.

Many formerly married and now remarried couples find themselves in situations where they are asked to counsel couples contemplating divorce. Many of these people are qualified counselors with busy professional practices. A

To Love Again

number of men whom I interviewed were former pastors whose denomination no longer allowed them a pastorate. Rather than sink into oblivion, they have gone into a counseling practice, feeling that they had much to offer out of their own heartbreak and pain. The possibility of extending help and hope to others in difficult and traumatic circumstances showed itself, and they were quick to respond. Their counseling is now more than theoretical; it is based on their own heartrending experiences. They are truly fighting to help preserve the Christian home; they are working to restore relationships, not just the institution of marriage. And God is blessing their efforts.

Because I had the nerve to write a book on the subject of divorce, I have often been asked to help counsel individuals contemplating divorce. It's never easy. I shall share one such counseling situation that happened in the initial stages of reading, studying, compiling questionnaire responses, and thinking and praying about what I would say in this book.

A young man in his mid-thirties—I'll call him Jim—met me after a morning church service. "I want you to go talk to my wife," he said.

The pastor who had been counseling Jim and Mitzi had already seen me, suggesting that I prayerfully consider talking to the couple. "Especially Mitzi," he said.

Mitzi had walked out of the marriage—something more and more women are doing today. It seems their options are greater—they have good-paying jobs, cars; some of them are finely educated and highly skilled in their professions. Circumstances don't look as bleak for women as they used to. Even ten or fifteen years ago, it was more difficult for women to think about a divorce. But times change.

My husband and I discussed the matter. It wasn't that I was unwilling to talk to either Mitzi or Jim, but I felt a restraining hand. We agreed that if Mitzi phoned and asked to see me, I should talk to her. In the meantime, we began praying, and several others did the same, asking God if this was His will, to impress upon Mitzi that *she* needed to seek me out. We waited and prayed four months. She had just read my book, *The Other*

Side of Divorce, and wanted to talk to me. Then the call came. The book did not contribute to her decision to walk out of the marriage; she didn't read it until she was four months into her separation. A few nights later, Mitzi came to our home where she and I could talk in private.

She was fidgety. (I'd seen that same restlessness before—this scene had been reenacted in different cities, different states, with different characters.) "What do you want out of life, Mitzi?"

It wasn't the question she'd expected. She was silent, contemplating. "Happiness."

(Sometimes the answer is "peace.")

"And you think on the other side of divorce you will find that?"

Sometimes the answer is yes. At other times it comes out, "Hopefully," or "Perhaps," or "I'm not sure."

Mitzi wasn't sure. That's always a hopeful sign. I like that answer best. It told me Mitzi wasn't sure she was making the right decision; she still had doubts; she was wavering. Divorce proceedings had begun, but it would still be a number of months before the divorce was final. To myself I thought: *Good, there's still time.*

You see, I do believe that God's prohibitions are meant for our own good, that He always has our best interests at heart and that His Word is meant to be obeyed. I conveyed these thoughts to Mitzi, adding, "God doesn't want to deprive any of us of *true* happiness or peace." I talked to her about what "true happiness" actually meant. We have such distorted ideas about what *happy* means. We become emotional cripples leaning all over each other, causing both our husbands (or our wives) and ourselves to fall, messing up our relationships because we live under the influence of a lie. We all think we have a right to happiness and that the person we're married to is morally obligated to create that happiness for us. Then when that doesn't happen and we don't receive from them what we think we are so deserving of, we shift all the blame on their failure to do the right things. We are quite literally in bondage to the actions of the person to whom we are married. Once we've

45

made up our minds about what happiness for us should consist of, and when it doesn't come our way quite the way we want it, we often take matters into our own hands. That does happen in many marriages; oftentimes there isn't a reciprocal effort on the part of each partner in the marriage. What we fail to recognize is that lasting and genuine happiness comes from within. It can't be *solely* dependent on outside influences— one's husband or wife, for instance.

That having been said, however, let it be acknowledged that the purpose of marriage, initially, as God ordered it, was to solve the problem of loneliness (see Gen. 2:18). Adams explains that the Bible explicitly speaks of marriage as *The Covenant of Companionship* (see p. 8, *Marriage, Divorce, and Remarriage in the Bible* by Jay E. Adams). The first couple's sin, however, marred that plan. So much, if not most, of the unhappiness marital partners experience is a result of trying to meet all their needs through this human relationship of marriage. Couples fail to meet each other's companionship needs; we live agonizingly lonely lives even within the bonds of marriage. What we have instead is legalized mating. The loving relationship between husband and wife that is to form the "one flesh" aspect of their marriage is missing. The loving relationship is important, of course, but we must also recognize that God, first of all, is *the* source of all happiness, contentment, and inner peace. But when there is so much conflict in a human relationship, for some there comes the breaking point. We desperately long for that loving, right relationship with our mate also.

The Apostle Paul wrote much about peace and being strengthened in the inner man through the abundant provision that God supplied. When he set down rules for holy living, he spoke of "clothing" ourselves with "compassion, kindness, humility, gentleness and patience" (Col. 3:12). He reminded his readers to bear with each other and to forgive whatever grievances they might have against one another. "Forgive as the Lord forgave you. And over all these virtues put on love, which binds them all together in perfect unity. Let the peace of Christ rule in your hearts, since, as members of one body, you were called to peace. And be thankful" (Col. 3:13*b*-15 NIV).

I spoke with Mitzi about the need to clothe oneself like that daily, and if necessary many times throughout the day. And we discussed what it means to have a thankful heart. I told her about a friend of longstanding who wrote telling of new insights he'd gained about himself by some serious introspection. He began to see how far he had fallen from what God desires from His children, and then he'd come into an understanding of the grace of God that was entirely new to him. The result brought exciting growth and change in his life and relationships. He was not the person he once had been. Although he felt he still had a long way to go, he was tremendously optimistic about the future. This friend had also experienced divorce and remarriage, and was experiencing some problems in his new marriage. But one of the things that helped him come to grips with himself before this marriage failed was an application of the Apostle Paul's words to his own life. This application had brought about unexpected and beautiful changes in his ability to handle the relationship.

This divorced-remarried man wrote: "Yes, I can look back on my life and point to some wrong choices that I have made. And if it were possible to live life over again, I would certainly do some things differently. But God lets us make mistakes; perhaps only through this way would I have come to the point where I now am. That's liberating."

I wonder if we in the Christian world have fully grasped this truth. Some of us made unwise marital choices; nevertheless, we made our way through the maze of problems, we grew along the way, but finally, for whatever reason—and there are many reasons—the struggle overwhelmed us and divorce became the unwanted option. The people whom I interviewed, and others who responded to the questionnaire, indicated that out of their marital failures they had grown. They felt liberated in more ways than merely loosening the bonds of marriage through divorce itself. Can we not stand alongside such as these and trust God to work through them to bring about such liberation in their thinking? Can we not accept that God is still at work in their lives?

And to the divorced person struggling with guilt and other disturbing emotions, can you accept that God hasn't deserted you? God could have intervened and stopped the first marriage from ever taking place. But He didn't. God will never force Himself on us, but He is in charge of circumstances.

We all need to acknowledge that there is such a thing as a wrong choice. The promise of God is that He makes all things, including our own wrong choices, work out for the good when we trust Him, and this includes divorced people who want to remarry.

I knew that one of several things could happen for Mitzi—for any of us—when we are confronted with seemingly impossible situations for which we see no reason to be thankful. "Thank God for who He is, Mitzi, and that you know He is able to make even this marital mess into something you will be able to continue to handle; or He will alter the circumstances; or you will find that His power is transforming you, giving you coping strength you never knew you had before."

I know there are those who would have counseled Mitzi to just praise and thank God and hang in there, that everything would turn out okay in her marriage. That's a very simplistic approach being foisted upon people in these terribly difficult marriage situations. I agree with counselor/writer John White, who says in his book *Parents in Pain,* that praise power, as it is currently taught and practiced, is a form of blasphemy. That it reduces God to a celestial vending machine. "Insert some praise, select the right button, then get whatever you want."[1] God can't be manipulated like that with any of our techniques, for He still sees the heart. And if our praise isn't genuine, it's as revolting as it is inappropriate.

In the first place, we aren't called on to praise God for evil. And there's a lot of evil in some marriages, even Christian marriages. And, as John White points out, in the second place, praise is to be an expression of trust and gratitude, not a technique for exerting pressure on God. So while the apostle Paul's injunction to "be thankful" is necessary and totally appropriate for the person suffering marital misery, the thankfulness is directed at who God is, at our understanding of

His faithfulness, His love, His mercy, and that we know He is able to bring good out of something evil. That kind of praise and thanksgiving is uplifting, purifying, and strengthening.

I told Mitzi what it's like on the other side of divorce for a Christian—the pain and the possibility. Perhaps I focused too much on the pain, but I wanted this young woman to fully understand that God's ideal is permanence in the marriage relationship. I was torn in my feelings because there were three beautiful children involved. These little ones needed their mother, yet I strongly suspected that since Mitzi had walked out of the marriage, the court would not look too favorably on her being granted custody of the children. I also doubted there would even be the option of joint custody.

In my book, *The Other Side of Divorce,* while I did not advocate divorce, I pointed out that I knew God could make the best of any regrettable situation, that His infinite love and boundless grace are able to redeem even the most tragic situation. I explained that while God hates divorce (Mal. 2:16), I John 1:9 applies to divorced people too. There we are told that if we confess our sins, He is faithful and just—He forgives us our sins, and cleanses us from *all* unrighteousness. I made this point clear to Mitzi.

I am convinced that disharmony in a relationship does not have to lead to the divorce court and that God can take even a little shred of love and rebuild that into a more beautiful love relationship than anything we could possibly imagine. I suggested to Mitzi that when she got home she write out the qualities she first admired in her husband, adding to it other qualities that had emerged through the years of their married life—that she write down the good things they had going for them—the deeper pleasures they had shared—the goals they had once mutually set out to reach.

I was quick to point out to her what I had observed in her husband—things that I thought were a real asset in any man, and that the moment she was free from him, there would be dozens of other women ready to latch onto him. Did she realize how few men there are in ratio to available women?

Many things came out of that conversation. Mitzi was on the

verge of getting a promotion on her job—she'd always worked in between giving birth to three babies, mothering them for awhile, and then leaving them with sitters to return to work. It was a practical necessity it seemed. Was her job totally satisfying? No, and she was beginning to understand that it might never be. Of course I was quick to tell her it would never be 100 percent what she wanted it to be, good as it might become. Some future travel was involved—I could tell her that after awhile all the airports and hotel rooms looked alike, the meetings were all quite similar, and home always seemed so good once I got back.

The major consideration, however, was her children. Mitzi had walked away from three children under the age of eight. This, to me, was a tragedy of unspeakable consequence, and I expressed my shock, my disapproval, my deep concern about the effects of that on the innocent children. She didn't like it when I talked that way; in fact, she protested. She hadn't walked away from the children; it was the unsatisfactory relationship with her husband, she explained. But, like it or not, the children had remained with her husband and she was seeing them now and then. They missed her terribly—just how much they missed her I was personally to see a few nights later when my husband and I called on her husband, and the youngest crawled on my lap and kept saying, "My mama is mad at me." On still another occasion, the child cried his heart out when it was time for bed. As a mother of four (and grandmother now of thirteen), I can pretty well determine what a certain cry means. Those cries were from deep within; they were not merely howls saying "I don't want to go to bed!" This child was grieving. (Later, I related these two incidents to Mitzi, and I saw *her* grieve.)

Divorce, I explained, carries with it a lot of pain and trauma that is not so easily seen before the divorce is final. It's ugly. Ugly to those involved and to onlookers who, although not necessarily directly involved, are, nonetheless, spectators in a sense—close enough to feel the pain, but not close enough to handle it the way we might like. It's especially ugly to children. And it's hard on other family members, too.

I talked about the cost of divorce in terms of: (1) finances, (2) emotions, (3) physical trauma, and (4) last, but certainly not least, the spiritual price one pays.

There is no way you can paint a pretty picture when you talk about divorce and *all* that is involved. It's a time of sadness, struggle, anguish, anxiety, and trauma.

"Count on it," I told her; "I know you've shed some tears already, but there will be lots more to come."

Mitzi was a sensitive young woman; I knew she would cry even more in the days ahead. I think I know what you are probably thinking—that a woman who would walk away from her children couldn't be too sensitive. But I've had to remind myself on this and on other occasions of a similar nature that we never know all the facts, and especially, as outsiders looking in (whether it's the church or us as individuals), in the final analysis, we don't really know what it's been like for the parties involved. (We haven't walked in their moccasins, as the old Indian saying goes!)

Later Mitzi was to tell me she wasn't so sure she was cut out to be a good mother, that in the frustrations of their marriage she often found herself taking out her unhappiness and frustration on her children. I admired her honesty about that. In fact, one of the primary reasons she gave for giving up the pretense and deciding to go for divorce, was her fear that she might end up harming one of the children. But I did tell her—as I would anyone making that statement—that even though she felt that way, it didn't cancel out the fact that *she was a mother.*

Then we talked about the future—what it might hold for her if she went through with the divorce. Were there some positives? Any bright possibilities? Some ray of hope? Happiness? Peace? Remarriage?

Remarriage.

What do you say to someone contemplating finalizing a divorce—someone young, intelligent, attractive—but someone who would have to help shoulder the burdens of tremendous financial problems that the divorce would impose upon both her and her husband? Someone who would give up her lovely home for a tiny one-bedroom apartment—who would struggle with depression, emotional and physical fatigue, and loneliness. Someone who would lose friends and experience alienation and the stigma that goes with it from those who would find themselves taking sides with her husband. And remarriage. Would that be a possibility for her?

Yes, how do you tell someone that divorce is not necessarily *the* answer, that remarriage may not become an option (statistically it's looking worse every year for women—available women far outnumber men). That she will have to face what the Bible says and work through that, and she will encounter severe criticism from other Christians.

Whenever there is a divorce involving young children, the problems and the pain are overwhelmingly real and difficult. In this instance, I had to remind Mitzi that even if she and Jim eventually married others, their problems with the children would be further complicated. There was a strong likelihood that they'd inherit some stepchildren. Had she thought about that? Was she prepared for the problems this might pose? And who was going to get custody of their three children? Would she and Jim be given joint custody? Would the court look favorably on her and grant custodial rights? Or would she end up only having visitation rights? Did she want to separate the children? Would that even be an option?

I'm sorry to have to tell you that five months after our conversation the divorce between Jim and Mitzi became final. Jim retained custody and was allowed to take the children with him to another state. Mitzi pays child support, and while she was given visitation rights, she is now separated from her children by thousands of miles.

It may seem to you that I was coming down too hard on Mitzi and that in some respects I was judging her too harshly. But I think I saw the handwriting on the wall, so to speak. My heart was broken for this family. I truly wished there were some way to put that marriage back together. But saving the institution of marriage just for the sake of the children does not always work out to the advantage of the children. These are hard situations. I have since seen Mitzi, and she appears at peace with herself.

Sad, but quietly serene. Theologically orthodox answers won't work in these difficult circumstances. There are no words. When I've seen her, I've embraced her, looked into her eyes and said, "I love you."

"I know you do," she has replied. "Thanks for helping me."

Help her? How did I help her? What did I say? I don't remember *all* that was said. I know I didn't just counsel her to run out and get the divorce. But I did assure her that God loves His children, and she assured me that she was one of those children. "Bear one another's burdens" (Gal. 6:2*a* NASB). I hope Mitzi and Jim sensed that what I was trying to do was to help them bear their burden—that I longed to spare them some of the future pain I knew would come as a result of the divorce. But I hope they also know that I believe with all my heart that even for each of them, and for their children, there exists the possibility for present and future happiness, forgiveness, and peace with God.

Divorce. Remarriage. To face reality is to recognize that what God demands of us is meant for our own good. God wants happiness for His children; He is prepared to give it. We do suffer consequences for our actions and for some wrong choices—it is the old law of sowing and reaping. What are we to make of all this? Are we to stay in miserable marriages? If we do divorce, are we to give up the idea of ever having another happy relationship? Is remarriage out for the Christian who doesn't have one of the biblical reasons for divorce? Do we have to reap a harvest of despair forever after?

Notes

1. John White, *Parents in Pain* (Downers Grove, Ill.: InterVarsity Press, 1979), p. 51.

Chapter Four

REMARRIAGE
A Harvest of Despair or Ongoing Fruitfulness?

As I said in my preface, strong and healthy second marriages are raising many perplexing questions for the church today. The prognostications of gloom and warnings of severe divine discipline are not necessarily coming true. To be sure, the individuals experienced heartache and problems that had to be worked out as a result of their divorces, but they have survived and moved on into fruitful living.

GRACE AND COMPASSION

In his book *Remarriage: A Healing Gift From God,* Larry Richards explains that in Jesus' kingdom there is a new way for us to function as Christians. It is the way of the King, and its name is Grace. Richards says:

Grace is a very difficult concept for the human mind to master. . . . Grace comes to us with forgiveness and with a promise. Grace does not threaten us, but says simply, "Love me. Let me work in your life. And I will make you a new and different person. I will lift you to be what you desperately want to be but have found that you cannot be."

Grace always seems to make ridiculous statements just like these. Grace always seems to ask us to accept the reality of our failures and our needs, inviting us to turn away from threats as motivation to choose the good and let God's love work a change within us.[1]

This is what I call compassionate theology. We apply our theological understanding of sin, grace, and the creation of human beings with sexual and companionship needs not only to marriage, but also to divorce and remarriage. The Gospels show us Jesus as a compassionate individual whose most attractive quality was that he "cared." Jesus accepted the challenge of grappling with issues that shaped the destinies of individual lives. Jesus, the Son of God, was and is love in action.[2] I don't see how Christians and the church can do anything less than to follow His example.

UNDERSTANDING THE REASONS FOR DIVORCE

None of the divorced-remarried individuals I interviewed were "lusting after evil," nor were they "setting their hearts on evil things" (see chapter 2), as is so often assumed and implied by the church. They were just simply people who didn't have the biblical "out" but had sub-ideal marriages. Tired of living a lie and putting on a false front, they decided to give up the pretense, hopeful that on the other side of divorce there was some degree of happiness and peace for them also. They felt that they'd had more than their share of the ugliness of a rotten relationship.

We have no way of knowing just how many Christians this involves these days. But as one Christian psychologist told me, "We can't ignore divorced Christians any longer in the Christian community—there are just too many of them; neither can we ignore divorced-remarried Christians—their numbers are really increasing!"

Many marriages are breaking up today because the husband is a practicing homosexual, and wives are calling a stop to the pretense of their marriage. In some instances, husbands are divorcing their wives for the same reason. I know of such a situation that occurred in a Nashville church we attended. The wife preferred her lesbian relationship. But this sort of thing is happening all across the country. Barbara Johnson, founder of Spatula Ministries, which deals with the increasingly prevalent homosexual problem in this country, relates that she is counseling more and more Christians caught in situations like this. The Christian community generally does not want to acknowledge this is a problem in its midst, but the truth is, it *is* a problem; it *does* exist. In many instances, a man and woman's relationship has been a marriage in name only, a convenience so the man can maintain his homosexual relationships and not be suspected (the situation is more common among men in the Christian community, it appears, than among women). Some of these men have been pillars in the Christian community— on our Christian college campuses, in the music field . . . highly respected, greatly admired. . . . The hidden anguish that their wives had to bear, alone and lonely, is beyond my comprehension. Yet many have stayed married. Why? Because of the resulting stigma of divorce and the attitude of the church toward remarriage. There were financial pressures and children to consider, and always the desire not to bring disrepute on the name of Christ.

If only those who haven't gone through a divorce could know the anguish divorced Christians experience, I somehow have to feel they would be less judgmental. It is so easy to talk about putting a marriage back together, becoming reconciled, laying aside your personal feelings, thinking of your children . . . ad infinitum . . . when you have a neat and tidy relationship. I think of several marriages where the couples were on the verge of divorce but did succeed in rebuilding their relationships. It *can* happen, and praise God when it does. But what happens so often is that churches, the clergy, others who haven't experienced the peculiar agony of a bad marriage and *all* the ramifications of that, just assume that because reconciliation has taken place for some, it should happen for all.

Why doesn't reconciliation happen for all? Many factors enter in. Sometimes it comes down to a basic willfulness on the part of one or both of the principles involved to go through with the divorce because they are unwilling, in the final analysis, to submit fully to God.

Those of us who are divorced and remarried don't like to hear that implied in a blanket sort of way, i.e., that this is everyone's problem. Generalizations such as that are commonly bandied about in many of the books on the subject, or expressed thoughtlessly by those who have little understanding or feeling for divorced people.

As I talked to Jim and Mitzi, for instance, I pointed out the need for submission first of all to God, and then a *mutual* submission to each other. It is not my point in this book to belabor this—whole books have been written on the subject. There are divergent views, some of which are very disturbing. Many of the writers show an entrenched obvious Christian male bias. Others are trying to help clear up confusion and get the reader to understand what the Ephesians 5:21-33 and Colossians 3:12-19 passages are actually saying.

The point is, that mutual submission unto the Lord—a true humbling of ourselves before God—is *the* building block upon which a solid marriage relationship exists. Once that happens, then other problem aspects of the marriage can be discussed that have been so destructive in the relationship. If that does not happen, for whatever reason, and mutual submission to God and to each other does not occur, even if the couple were to go back together (if the church, for instance, successfully aided in reuniting a couple), it would still be a marriage in name only. And that's what so many Christian couples today are facing and are unwilling to prolong. An other-person-centered relationship is what it comes down to. Marriage needs to have Christ at *the* center, and then a focus, individually, on the welfare and best interests of the other. What many women have related to me is that the church insisted on a sort of blind submission and obedience to their husbands without the recognition that these Bible passages have much, or more, to say to husbands as well.

Christians contemplating divorce or remarriage need to study these passages and ask themselves if they are really measuring up, and if they are prepared to measure up in another try at marriage. If they will honestly confront themselves, and then make the changes that are necessary, there is no doubt in my mind that many marriages could be saved. So often, however, one or the other (or both) of the parties involved insists that the other person change. The result is a contest of the wills, usually hopelessly deadlocked, that doesn't make for a good marriage, let alone harmonious Christian living!

So often divorced individuals say they can't understand why their prayers aren't being answered. This is especially true when the divorce is in progress, and the one who didn't instigate the divorce is struggling, hoping against hope that his wife (or her husband) won't go through with the proceedings. Jim, for instance (mentioned in the previous chapter), a deacon in his church, couldn't understand why Mitzi wasn't coming back to him and the children. So many were praying; he was praying. I asked him if he felt he had been living considerately with Mitzi, if he had been dealing with her in an understanding way, coming at the problems in their relationship with an awareness of her perspective (see I Pet. 3:7). He wasn't familiar with this verse and couldn't give me an answer, skillfully avoiding a response. I've asked that question of others. Most people don't want to admit they are at fault to any great degree. But the answer can be found in this verse where it says a husband is to treat his wife with reverence so that his prayers may *not* be hindered. But wives don't get off easily here either; earlier verses tell them how to behave. "Your godly lives will speak to them better than any words" (I Pet. 3:2 TLB). It's a case of actions speaking louder (and better) than words.

Sometimes couples talk too much. They argue. Fight. On the other side of the coin, however, are those couples who don't communicate at all. In both cases, it is probably quite safe to say that neither the arguing, talkative couple, nor the noncommunicating couple are, in fact, really communicating.

One man said, "I think the big difference in my remarriage is that we are trying to do things God's way where each of us, as a part of the marriage team, is committed to doing what God's Word has to say, and we don't hold ourselves responsible for the mistakes we see in the other person. *We hold ourselves responsible only for how we react to those mistakes,* and if our reactions are right, everything else is manageable."

CHANGE AND ACCEPTANCE

Many marriages break down at this very point—where one of the marriage partners is so hung up on the idea of the other person changing that nothing and no one can get through to him or her.

It is not that changes aren't necessary. But where do people begin to try to help their mates in recognizing this without alienating them? Sometimes the mates become so defensive that there isn't anything, it seems, that one can do or say that doesn't bring forth a mouthful of defensiveness. Defensive people are very difficult to live with over the long haul.

But the place to begin changing is with yourself. The first help a couple can actually give each other is acceptance—mutual acceptance as between equals. You begin by being the kind of changed person, in every way, that you would like your mate to become. But stubbornness, pride, selfishness, immaturity—Jesus called it hardness of heart—do surface, and such basic self-centeredness is not conducive to an honest exchange of communication. This problem surfaced in questionnaire responses to a large degree. So the church must recognize that self-centeredness is a terribly real problem.

A good illustration came from one gentleman who confessed that in the twenty-nine years of his first marriage, all he looked for were changes he'd like to see take place in his wife. He was never willing to look at himself. Some years after his wife divorced him, he remarried. Within a very short period of time, he made the devastating discovery that his second marriage wasn't faring any better than the first, that he couldn't force his second wife to change and do what *he* thought God says a wife should do in a marriage.

"It was only when I quit saying, 'What is the matter with her?' and began to say, 'What is the matter with me?' that things began to turn around. I had to learn again the hard way, and it took about three years before I realized this.

"The very day I asked myself, 'I wonder if I am the culprit who was in charge of the demolition of my first marriage, and I wonder if I am the one who is actually causing the problems that I now face'; it was that very day that I began to look at it like that, that it was almost as if God said, 'Well, that is better; now we can do something about this marriage.' "

After that, it didn't take long and he was able to progress to the place where he promised God and himself, and eventually discussed the matter with his second wife, that he would not try to force her into any conduct, or standard of living which she herself did not adapt to on her own. He still reserved the right to point out to her what he felt God's Word had to say on a given subject, "But even that was not very well accepted," he admits, "and I finally had to take a hands-off attitude, and just leave her and our situation in the hands of God. I had to take my own life in tow and look at myself in the light of the Word of God.

"The ugly facts are, as far as I am concerned, that I discovered that I had failed in every category the Bible lays down as being the rules by which a successful marriage must be lived (if it is to be acceptable to God, and acceptable to each other). I not only had to admit that to myself, but the day came when I had to tell my wife I had failed. I had to take total responsibility as the husband, and only when I did that, was God able to step into our picture and begin to set things straight."

This pastor who is also a marriage counselor is of the opinion that the growing divorce rate is because of the ignorance on the part of those who were married. "They are ignorant of what God requires for a marriage. God designed marriage; it is His institution. He laid down the ground rules both for husbands and wives. Because we are ignorant of those basic principles, and are constantly violating them, we throw stress into the marriage relationship that it was not designed to bear. There are many factors involved in individual cases, but the average Christian is almost totally unaware of what God says is necessary for a marriage to exist happily."

This was underscored in other responses to the questionnaire—the idea that we come into our marriages with unrealistic expectations, and that many second marriages succeed because experience is a good teacher when we honestly, like the pastor-counselor mentioned, will confront our own shortcomings and submit to God. Of course, it must be acknowledged that many second marriages are no better than the first-time failures.

LEARNING FROM FAILURE

Persons I contacted, and statistics in general, show that even though divorce is painful and remarriage is risky, the need to be married overruled, and they were willing to discount the risks. Five out of six divorced men, for instance, marry again. Husbands and wives agreed that their second marriages were better than their first. A commonly expressed comment is, "I should have married my second wife (or husband) the first time." There was a strong current of contentment flowing in these second-time-around marriages. Lessons had been learned; changes had been made; forgiveness of God had been sought—there was a lot of determination to make the new marriage succeed and faith enough to believe that God hadn't deserted them.

Two individuals had failed second marriages. One woman's husband had died, and she remarried too soon. "Sometimes I feel like I'm living in a soap opera," she wrote. "I didn't like being single, but I think I was married too long and too happily (if that's possible). So after being happily married most of my adult life, I was terribly lonely. I realized that I didn't care for the man who became my second husband as I cared for my first husband, but I honestly felt that I could not care for another man in that same way. It was a little over two years after George's death that I remarried. It was much too soon—at least for me.

"What went wrong? I firmly believe that a widowed or divorced person should not remarry too quickly. Marriage—whether the first or second time, but especially the second time around—should be approached with 'fear and trembling,' and an unlimited supply of 'agape' love. Having loved and lived so happily before, I believed, and still believe, I have much to bring to a marriage. However, having married so young I was very naïve about men. My second husband was an alcoholic—something I did not suspect at all while we were going together. This came as a terrible shock to me. He became physically violent after drinking, and I found that I could not live in fear. I

61

realized too late that the person I married was not the person I thought he was. Our divorce was not by mutual agreement. He tried to win me back, and I would have been willing to reconsider if we had gone for counseling. However, he would not do this, and I knew that I could not live the rest of my life with an alcoholic.

"I know I have grown as a result of first becoming a widow, and now having gone through divorce. . . ."

Another woman, now happily remarried for a third time—with this marriage into its fourteenth year—is now involved with her husband, in a church that accepted them and asked them to help with divorced singles. Someone asked this third-time-around remarried woman how she got from where she was to where she is today, and all she could say was, "A day at a time!" It hadn't been easy, but she had come to understand how broad God's mercies are compared to our narrowmindedness.

"Seven months after leaving my second husband, in desperation I cried out to God. Of course, He'd been waiting for me to do that! But now, in this marriage, there's a deep commitment to making it work. We both work hard at communication—something we feel is so vital to a good relationship. God has redeemed my mistakes of the past—I couldn't and I can't. And none of us can make up for mistakes with one spouse through another. But praise God! I believe in miracles, and this marriage is one. Jesus Christ is truly the head of our home. For me, this began when I gave Him complete control; then I was able to go on, having accepted His forgiveness for past failure, and not live in guilt and with condemnation."

Does past failure disqualify us from receiving God's blessing and help? That is actually a foolish question. Yet the persistent reaction to remarried Christians sometimes leaves you with the impression that a first-time marital failure takes you out of the sphere of God's love and renders you incapable of sustaining a new relationship. In fact, it was their very failures that made so many interviewees determine that with God's help they would redeem the breakup of the first marriage by establishing a stable emotional relationship with someone else.

"I came through the divorce deeply wounded," one woman said. "The wounds left by that traumatic experience were a long time in healing. To this day, the scars remain. But the scars only remind me that I'll never let it happen again. Others were wounded and scarred too. As a result of this knowledge, both my second husband and I are growing together. There's something so much better about this marriage. I can't quite put my finger on it—I do know we both have a deep commitment both to God and to each other to make it succeed."

M. W., a former pastor, now involved in a singing-counseling ministry, admitted that he hadn't prepared for marriage the first time. He was in the army, lonesome, and thought he had found the right girl—she was supplying a need, friendship. "I was dumb enough to ask her to marry me without consulting the Lord, but we did go through some premarital counseling; however, it just didn't hold up. I had not given marriage all the thought that I needed to. I acted impulsively. I expected my marriage would be as great as I knew my Mom and Dad's was, and then when it fizzled, it hurt. But I didn't give up easily; I recognized that good could still come out of the relationship. I realized, however, that the marriage was wrong six months after we married when she said that she wanted a divorce. I was troubled after that, and it became more apparent when we started keeping score—you know, a ten-dollar present for my Mom, then a little over ten dollars for her Mom, that kind of silly thing, but we could never resolve our differences. This went on for ten years."

It was while he was pastoring a very successful church that his wife said one day, "If you think our marriage is so crummy, why don't we just get a divorce?" Off and on they had thrown this at each other, but that time it hit.

"I'm sick and tired of this," he said. "I'm tired of playing games with the congregation thinking everything is so hunky-dory when it is not. I'm also very tired of hearing this business, 'Let's get a divorce,' and of seeing my little girl go through the struggles our constant arguing is having upon her."

At that point he decided to take off a couple of weeks. He wanted to be alone. "I made the decision during that time that I wasn't going to go on like that anymore," he related.

Of course he was devastated by his church's reaction to his decision. "You are supposed to stick it out, and keep going no matter what—ministers especially—and that was the category I fit into then."

Then he added, "I don't know how your book can help the church, to be perfectly honest. I'm not so sure many churches want any help, that they think divorced people deserve a second opportunity.

"But I hardly believe I am the same guy today, the transition in my thinking has been tremendous. When I was totally honest with God, the way He has worked in my life is just . . . well, just thinking about it brings tears, because I tell you, it has been wonderful what God has done. If I had stayed in the first marriage I'd still be the same guy today I was then—miserable, out of fellowship with God even though I had everyone thinking everything was okay, and both my first wife and I were miles apart, even though we lived in the same house. As I have striven to be a doer of God's Word, to take and submit only to those things that are in harmony with what He says, the transformation has been total, not perfect, not completed, but oh my, it is an amazing thing. I look back and wish I'd had half of the Christian graces, and of these new understandings to begin with—things might have been so different. But hindsight is better than no sight, so I thank God daily for what's happened to me, and my remarriage is great."

WHERE THE CHURCH FAILS

This man's story reminds me of Dale Galloway's heart-wrenching account in *Rebuild Your Life* of how he, as a successful pastor, went through the divorce trauma. His wife left him, taking their two children with her. He lost not only his marriage, but his ministry and, for a time, his peace. The fact that both M. W. and Dale Galloway loved God with all their hearts and wanted more than anything else to be used in His service didn't seem to matter to their respective churches. The circumstances that brought about their divorces weren't even considered. They were divorced ministers, and their churches branded them as failures in the ministry. To the officials of each man's denomination, they were done, washouts, with no way to ever return to the position of pastoring one of their denomination's churches. Such was the blanket sentence passed on these two clergymen, a sentence that is not at all unusual to most conservative churches.

Galloway urges the reader to put his or her failures behind and move ahead. "Today my heart bleeds for the multitudes of men who have been washed out of their churches. Who, yes, have failed, but worse yet, have been branded failures forever. The church of Jesus Christ must be more redemptive than this."[3] To which I can only add a hearty "Amen," as would others in a similar situation.

Galloway did go on to rebuild his life, to remarry, to love again, and to become founder and pastor of Portland's New Hope Community Church, where he has a dynamic ministry that is dedicated to healing hurts and building dreams. M. W. also went on to rebuild, to remarry, and to love again. But both these men went through a lot of needless heartache when their churches wiped out their credibility with their denomination. Is it any wonder that M. W. said he wasn't so sure some of these churches want any help, or that they think divorced people deserve a second opportunity?

In I Timothy 3 we are told that not only must a pastor be the husband of one wife, but he must have a well-behaved family, with children who obey quickly and quietly (v. 4 TLB). The question is asked, "For if a man can't make his own little family behave, how can he help the whole church?" (v. 5 TLB). In other words, he is to manage his entire household well, keeping his children under control with all dignity (V. 4 NASB). If we are going to be consistent in the exercising of church discipline (a subject further discussed in chapter 5), then it would seem we have a lot of housecleaning to do in churches throughout the land. Some of the people who are having the most difficulty in raising their children and in managing them, are pastors, a fact that the Christian world tends to ignore. For some reason, pastors with this kind of a problem get off the hook, but the pastor who goes through a divorce does not. This seems to me to be a glaring inconsistency. Furthermore, it could be pointed out that deacons *likewise* (see v. 8 NASB) must be the same sort of good, steady men as the pastors. That *likewise* is important; it refers to what was just said about pastors and their families. Some of the deacons who are the most vocal about divorce and remarriage need to take care of their family life before stepping out to point fingers at the divorced or divorced-remarried in their midst.

SCARS TRANSFORMED INTO BEAUTY

Christy, a beautiful, slim, dark-haired young woman in her late thirties, had been divorced nine years before she remarried. She harbored a lot of guilt and felt if she remarried she'd be living in sin for the rest of her life. (A common fear among many Christians.) How did she respond to that?

"There was a period of time that I rebelled. I threw caution to the wind and decided if the church was going to brand me, and if God couldn't countenance remarriage, what hope was there for me anyway? I enjoyed dating and being in the company of men—I wasn't cut out to be a single all my life, and I recognized that. So I just did a lot more dating, but I couldn't find the kind of companion I knew I really wanted and needed outside the church. I wanted to remarry a Christian and finally cleared up my thinking about the matter. I, like you, Helen, decided to throw myself on God's mercy, trusting Him for forgiveness and the right to make a new life for myself."

Christy began attending church with a greater degree of faithfulness. Then one day she attended a singles function at the church and met her husband-to-be, a widower. They began dating and it was obvious almost from day one that the two were meant for each other. My husband and I had the joy of living across the street from Christy and Lyle when they married. From the way Christy spoke Lyle's name each time we visited, the way they looked at each other and reached for each other's hand, I knew theirs was an especially rich relationship, sanctioned and blessed by God. Rarely have I seen a more beautiful relationship.

How do you explain this joyous happiness, this radiant woman who exudes such devotion to her second husband? Christy participates in the choral activities of their church. Should she be denied that right because she did not have one of the three commonly accepted reasons for divorce? Lyle is a Bible teacher, a loyal, hard worker in the church. But he is married to a divorced woman. According to some Christians, Christy and Lyle are supposed to be reaping a harvest of despair. The Christys and Lyles are to be found in churches across our land. If remarriage is so wrong, then someone better rise up and explain what we see happening. Christy's son now has a godly stepfather; Lyle's daughter now has a loving stepmother—a godly woman to provide this growing girl with the kind of nurturing a teenager needs.

Churches anxious to express the highest ideals of God rather than meet the raw realities of life may feel they have to legislate against remarriage of individuals divorced without one of the biblical reasons. It would seem, by contrast, that people who have gone through the breakup of a first marriage, and then have remarried, need the spiritual support the church can help provide, if they are to thrive once more for the Lord.

More than one theologian writing on this points out that the Bible doesn't authorize us to distinguish between the innocent and guilty parties, according to Matthew 5:32 and 19:9, in the matter of remarriage. In an article about remarriage, George W. Peters says, "If this seems too permissive, we must not forget that it is Christ who speaks or who does not speak. His silence here is difficult to interpret. Yet, He is the all-wise One. We must not make His silence into positive permission nor turn it into negative legislation."[4]

This theologian cautions about reading our sentiments and judgments into the silence of Christ and the Apostle Paul. Likewise, he cautions about placing our judgment and wisdom above the wisdom of the Creator who said, "It is not good that the man should be alone; I will make him an help meet for him" (Gen. 2:18 KJV).

Peters continues, "Forgiveness, reconciliation, and restoration are preferable and far more ideal. However, if these are not possible, divorce and remarriage cannot be forbidden on the basis of the words of Christ or on the teaching of Paul."

Peters cautions about minimizing the sin of divorce with all its evil consequences and judgments when it takes place for reasons other than those stated in Matthew 5:32; 19:9; and I Corinthians 7:15. But this theologian strongly affirms that "it does not place those involved in such remarriage outside of forgiveness if repentance takes place, nor does it demand dissolution of the second marriage."[5]

Some scars cannot be transformed into beauty; as Peters points out, they remain scars, but divorced-remarried Christians need all the help that the church can provide.

The pastor-counselor quoted elsewhere in this chapter made this provocative statement, in response to my questionnaire: "Actually my reply may sound very selfish, and I hope it will be understandable to your readers, but the rewards of my remarriage as I look at it and realize what has taken place, have been a tool that God has used to straighten out my own sense of values. I would be willing to go through the heartache again, if necessary, to achieve the new sense of spiritual well-being that I now feel. Again I emphasize, divorce is not God's better way of achieving this. . . ."

This man and other interviewees emphasized that in their second marriages they had found themselves. They found what God expects of them in their remarriage relationship, and they are still learning. All agreed that divorce is not the best way to find this out, but that experience is a very good teacher, if not the most severe teacher.

I have said before in *The Other Side of Divorce* that divorce is not necessarily a solution. It's not easy. It's hurtful. It's ugly. It's costly. It's painful. But sometimes it is necessary to save your sanity. One man picked up on that and added, "Like having a leg removed, that, too, may be necessary, but it leaves you a cripple. I can't find anything good in divorce except to say that Romans 8:28 includes even that . . . 'all things work together for good to them that love God.' . . . But we are working with very difficult and painful things, and the later in life divorce happens, the more devastating it seems. However, *all things are possible with God.* I do know my relationship to Him, to the church, to my fellow Christians, and to the world, has been greatly improved. God has used these tragic mistakes of mine to enrich my life, but I wish that I had learned it by another route. I wish I would have not disgraced myself and disgraced God's Word. I have found people who mocked God because of what happened in my life. Put it like this, when you fall from a flagpole as high as the one on which my flag was flying, you will find more people shooting at you than saluting you."

This kind of attitude was expressed again and again from the individuals I interviewed and those who responded to the questionnaire. One man who has an extensive premarital, marriage, and counseling ministry, stated: "I have been in a growing process ever since the divorce took place. I know that I am forgiven by God. If it wasn't for the grace of God, I don't know where I would be. I entered into the divorce with a whole lot of prayer, and I just kept right on going. I knew that I wasn't living up to God's ultimate in my first marriage. I knew that getting a divorce wouldn't be living up to His ideal either, but since the divorce, unbelievable things have happened, and I get excited about that. I know it isn't within God's perfect plan for people to destroy each other in a bad marriage relationship.

"I entered into my second marriage with a whole lot of prayer, too. Jesus told the woman who was caught in the act of adultery, 'Neither do I condemn thee: go, and sin no more' (John 8:11 KJV). If I sinned in remarrying, I repent of my sin. God said He would not condemn those who come to Him genuinely repentant, seeking His forgiveness. He has shown us He reconciles relationships through His Son, Jesus Christ, and the relationship that needed reconciling in my life, above anything else, was my relationship with my heavenly Father. It was being destroyed in my first marriage; it has been restored. The greatest thing that I have seen in the Bible is this: 'But now abide faith, hope, love, these three; but the greatest of these is love' (I Cor. 13:13 NASB). I possess these three things; God does that for us. I have faith to believe that what He promises in His Word is true—even for divorced-remarried people. I experience His love daily, and the hope I have placed in Him never disappoints me. That hope says there is something out there for divorced-remarried people. No, we don't have to reap a harvest of despair; there can be ongoing fruitfulness for us."

Notes

1. Larry Richards, *Remarriage: A Healing Gift From God* (Waco, Tex.: 1981), p. 57.

2. As a result of fully understanding this—personally experiencing the compassion of Christ—I wrote a book entitled *The Caring Jesus,* which has since been retitled *Jesus: Love in Action.*

3. Dale E. Galloway, *Rebuild Your Life* (Wheaton, Ill.: Tyndale House Publishers, 1981), p. 83.

4. From *Moody Monthly* magazine, "What the Bible Says About Divorce," by G. W. Peters, © 1971 MBI. Reprinted with permission. A full discussion of his views on the subject can be found in the Moody Press booklet, *Divorce and Remarriage.*

5. Ibid., p. 43.

Chapter Five

Failure, Guilt, and the Church

Is there a time when a church should discipline a person for divorce? How can the church administer discipline to divorced and remarried couples?

Stanley E. Ellisen, Professor of Biblical Literature at Western Conservative Baptist Theological Seminary, in Portland, Oregon, points out that scrambled eggs cannot be unscrambled, but a remarried couple can be rededicated as they are to God. Remarriage is definitely a salvage operation in a number of ways, and salvaging the family is definitely a part of the program of our redemptive God.

Remarriage then is to be regarded as a new life and redemptive experience. It is not to be lived with compunctions of guilt and a haunted conscience of regrets, but to be accepted as a new experience in the perfect will of God. God's concern after their repentance has taken place is that the new couple pick up the pieces, put it all together with divine help, and move on from there. This was doubtless part of the mission of Jesus as He visited the home of the Samaritan woman for two days in John 4, for only the one she then lived with could have become her husband. The Lord is in the salvaging business, and the rebuilding of half-destroyed homes is part of that program. It is essential that we recognize this redemptive aspect of remarriage and never underestimate the grace and power of God in this home-reconstruction business. And if it is His business, it ought to be ours.[1]

I have not found a more concise statement reflecting compassionate theology than these words by Dr. Ellisen.

DISCIPLINE AND THE CHURCH

A question that arises in connection with the church's discipline relates to whether or not divorced or divorced-remarried individuals have any right to participate in service as deacons, elders, teachers, singing in the choir, or even serving as a pastor. Dr. Ellisen's comments, I believe, provide guidelines. He says:

The crucial issue is not [the remarried person's] history, but their character; not their past, but their present. *Their history is indeed important where it reveals impenitence and an unwillingness to acknowledge their failure in a marriage breakup.* Such have not learned the lesson of their failure and will only propagate their failure in others. *Where such repentance and confession have not occurred accompanied by a change in character and spiritual stability, they definitely are not qualified to represent the church in public service.* Where this change has taken place, however, that person's qualifications and character should be evaluated in the light of that change. God is able to use an unfaithful apostle Peter after restoration to reach out with sympathy to other unfaithful people. He delights to salvage broken things and put them into productive service. He did that with murderous Saul of Tarsus, adulterous Augustine, and Mary Magdalene, to mention but a few outstanding examples. Salvaging personalities and homes is His specialty.[2] (Italics mine.)

When should the church administer discipline? The answer must be, as Dr. Ellisen points out, when the individual is impenitent, when there is no evidence of a change of character and spiritual stability. What about cases where the couple does show maturity and a regard for spiritual things? Let me tell you how a school handled our case.

When my husband applied for a position with a Christian school, he had to appear before the school board. This would have been necessary for anyone applying for the position; in our case, there was an added dimension—Herman and I were divorced-remarried individuals. So not only did my husband have to appear before the school board for the usual questions, but he was also asked about the divorce and the remarriage. Then it was my turn. Because this was a Christian school, the proper steps were being taken to ensure that we were, indeed, right with the Lord.

Later, when we moved to the southern part of the United

States, my husband once again submitted to what some might call an interrogation, as it were. In each of these instances, we provided names and addresses of places where we had worked before, and people who knew us well. Some of these people we knew might not have approved of divorce, or of remarriage; nevertheless, we supplied accurate information. Were we at any point concerned? Basically, we were trusting the Lord to work on our behalf; however, we faced the reality that individuals are fallible and that many in the Christian world have difficulties accepting remarriage. If, at any point, after hiring my husband, these people had discovered that his character didn't match up with his testimony, and that there wasn't spiritual stability, then they would have been right in administering discipline.

Larry Richards (*Remarriage: A Healing Gift from God*) reminds us that law came through Moses. Grace came through Jesus. Sometimes the reality of our lives fails to match the ideal to which the church is committed. Richards asks, "How does God deal with such failures?" and answers, "In terms of the persons involved, by counseling the way of greatness."[3]

We should reread Ephesians 4:32—a verse I have used with consistency since my divorce and remarriage, have pointed out to critics, and whose words I have advised the walking wounded to use as they respond to their accusers. The apostle Paul tells us, "Be kind and compassionate to one another, forgiving each other, just as in Christ God forgave you" (NIV).

When we were criticized following our marriage, I would sometimes remind my husband, as well as myself, that we didn't have to look at the little fingers pointed against us, but instead we should look at the great arm that was for us. Those who see the great arm of God need not fear ten thousand little fingers. Real friends don't need explanations, and our enemies won't believe us anyway, so we shouldn't bother with self-defense. We should let God fight our battles (see Romans 12:19).

Larry Richards emphasizes that the church shouldn't erect more rigid rules to try to control behavior, that we should trust our brothers and sisters to respond to God, and the church can best help them respond by giving support and by extending forgiveness. He says, "We are to take the mantle of grace and mercy worn so comfortably by Jesus and to wrap that mantle around ourselves and our brothers. . . . any retreat to law is in some sense a denial of grace. . . . Truth, grace, and mercy all testify to God's compassionate motives in permitting, through the Old Testament age and even today, remarriage as his direct and guided will for some of his children."[4]

God hasn't made any of us judges over other human beings. The book of James says: "Don't criticize and speak evil about each other, dear brothers. If you do, you will be fighting against God's law of loving one another, declaring it is wrong. But your job is not to decide whether this law is right or wrong, but to obey it. Only he who made the law can rightly judge among us. He alone decides to save us or destroy. So what right do you have to judge or criticize others?" (James 4:11-12 TLB).

THE PROBLEM OF GUILT

Without a doubt, one of the biggest problems facing the formerly married and the divorced-remarried relates to handling guilt. Just about the time you think you've licked the problem, something happens to make it resurface. It can be triggered by the inconsequential, as well as more significant events. To what extent has the church contributed to unnecessary guilt—especially that of divorced-remarried couples?

Dwight Hervey Small has something to say about this in his book, *The Right to Remarry:*

The extraordinary feature of God's redemptive work in Christ is that He freely offers pardon to all who come to Him in faith. The utter joy of being pardoned is that one is fully and forever freed from two things: guilt and penalty! But if God does not give divorced Christians reason for continuing guilt, *the evangelical Church most likely will!* If God does not exact a penalty, *the Church in many instances does!* Perhaps even more seriously, where one is the victim of divorce, of where divorce is solely the result of failure—not particular sin—the Church too eagerly treats it as though it were the result of sin. In the most demanding intimate relationship possible, the Church asks for success on the part of every couple, despite the evident fact that with respect to no ethical absolute of our Lord can the Church produce a community claiming such success. Thus it becomes a problem of the Church's unreal expectation. Idealistically, the Church proclaims the sufficiency of Christ and the power of the Holy Spirit for all human problems, and this sufficiency no true Christian would deny. . . . But realism forces us to come to terms with the limitations of Christian believers to appropriate the resources in God. . . . The question of God's sufficiency is not the relevant question; it is man's ability to appropriate the sufficiency of God's resources that is at issue.[5]

At the Christian bookseller's convention in Anaheim in the summer of 1984, I learned about a man who is struggling under a painful load of guilt. It seems his teenage son was the victim of a terrible accident. The boy's death was a staggering blow to the father, a divorced-remarried man. The question that haunts him now is this: Did God punish him for the divorce and remarriage by taking the life of his son?

I don't know the circumstances surrounding this man's first marriage, or whether he even instigated the divorce. But I don't need to know in order to hold out to him the assurance that even though there was failure in his first marriage, God doesn't deal with His repentant children in terms of extracting a penalty (in his case, the death of his son through an accident). Dwight Small emphasizes that Jesus' words regarding divorce do not place the failing Christian under the condemning status of a broken law. Where did this dear man ever get the idea that God is such a mean God that He would get even with him by having his son involved in an accident that would claim his life? I'm afraid the church has been responsible for instilling those kinds of thoughts and fears into the minds of her people, to a large degree.

Ray S. Anderson says: "If the church is such a thing as grace, then let the church be bold in grace. The stigmas that the church places upon those who bear the marks of sin have no existence in the sight of Christ."[6]

When God forgives, He removes the sin and our failure to live up to His stated standards, as far as the east is from the west. That's a *long* way. Can you measure it? "The Lord is merciful and gracious, slow to anger, and plenteous in mercy. He will not always chide: neither will he keep his anger for ever. He hath not dealt with us after our sins; nor rewarded us according to our iniquities. For as the heaven is high above the earth, so great is his mercy toward them that fear him. As far as the east is from the west, so far hath he removed our transgressions from us. Like as a father pitieth his children, so the Lord pitieth them that fear him" (Ps. 103:8-13 KJV).

This man (whose son was killed) has a beautiful, godly second wife. If ever a woman fit the Proverbs 31 definition of "a truly good wife" (see v. 10, especially TLB), this woman does. Someone has said, "Second wives, second best." You can take that several ways. This woman is *not* second best, believe me. And I know a lot of second wives who qualify as Proverbs 31 women. This man is blessed to have her as his wife. Is God punishing him for divorce and remarriage? I do not believe it. And I hope he reads this book and that it can be used to bring healing to his broken heart. There are many others like him—women as well as men—divorced, now remarried, carrying around a heavy burden of guilt. My plea to you is simply this: give that unnecessary burden to your heavenly Parent. Recognize that He has given you a new opportunity in this marriage to bring glory to Him.

I want to point the guilt-laden reader to Small's words, which I believe carry so much possibility for healing. He says:

What divorce often signifies is that a formal marriage was not in any sense a true marriage according to the design of God. In so many instances it would be difficult if not impossible to say, "What God has joined together." There are marriages, well intended at the start, which never realize any semblance of the unity of persons envisioned by the biblical concept. *The failure is not the divorce; the failure was the marriage itself.* To perpetuate the marriage may be only to perpetuate a lie. And to make it more may be beyond the capacity of the individuals involved, despite their Christian orientation. Any pastoral expectation is sheer unreality in such cases, and indicates the need for pastoral self-examination.

The justification for remarriage in God's sight must arise from the reality of grace. Remarriage is always related to the renewing grace of God, which meets a person in his or her failure and grants another chance. This is not only true of the "innocent party," but the "guilty party" as well. For grace to be grace means that there is no intrinsic justification at all, no "right" which enters the picture to guide our evaluation and action. It is not a matter of personal right, but of God's grace in Christ. . . . the right to remarry is neither a personal nor an absolute right at all; it is granted, not by the Creation orders, nor by the law of the Kingdom, but only by the grace of a forgiving Lord.[7]

So I find myself asking, does the church try to assume responsibility (discipline) for matters that it is not really responsible for? In my reading, I learned that the word *guilt* comes from the Anglo-Saxon word *gylt*, which means crime. It also indicates that guilt has something to do with sin and culpability (the fact of being culpable—deserving of blame, liable to blame). So, to be guilty of something bad is to be accountable and responsible for it.

We are back to square one: When and where does guilt begin in the case of divorced-remarried individuals? Can anyone answer that? Are any of us sure we are *fully* qualified to assign blame? Have we lived under the same roof, slept in their beds, participated in *their* daily routines?

We talk about unnecessary guilt and excessive guilt, both of which imply that there is such a thing as real guilt. But dwelling on past mistakes and rehashing all that contributed to marital failure certainly slows the healing process. Is it right of the church to drag everything out into the open and inflict this on divorced-remarried people who are attempting once again to establish a relationship and rebuild a Christian home?

I know of one church that confronted this problem. A man and a woman had run off together, leaving the husband of the woman and the entire church in a state of shock. The woman got a quickie divorce in another state, and she and the man were married. They didn't come back to the church; instead they found a new church home. What was the church to do where the husband remained? They decided the way of love demanded that they not try to exercise disciplinary measures on anyone. The husband who was left in the church had already suffered enough; he remained in the church, and it was in *his* best interests that the church rally around him with love. Some time later he remarried. Obviously, he had the biblical reason to remarry.

The church could have exercised disciplinary measures toward the man and woman who ran off together, and by so doing have created a messy problem. What would have been accomplished? If this man and woman, however, had attempted to reenter the life of the church, at that point, the church would have been remiss if it had not exercised discipline. Then, indeed, it would have made it difficult for the husband who remained and, in that instance, the church should have stood with the brother who had been wronged. Certainly, in this instance, guilt was clear, for the church cannot condone a woman's running off with another man while married. Practically all the situations I have encountered, however, among divorced-remarried people were not of this clear-cut nature; they were not deserving of censure or church discipline. Unfortunately, there are fine Christian men and women to be found in churches across the land—divorced-remarried individuals—who are being denied the right to serve on church boards, to teach, to sing in the choir.

I would imagine if we would each examine ourselves we would have to admit there is enough of failure there to occupy our time without pointing fingers at others. But is even that necessary? Certainly not if it's been confessed and has been forgiven—canceled through Christ's death. Isn't God greater than all our guilt—greater than deserved guilt? Why does God love us? Is it because we are so lovable and good?

REDEMPTIVE GRACE TRANSFORMS FAILURE

Some of God's greatest trophies of grace are those people who have failed him so miserably in the past. We can all think of numerous examples. Some of these people have become our Christian heroes and heroines in contemporary society. They were guilty of some very atrocious misdeeds and even heinous crimes, yet we have elevated them to a certain status in our Christian culture. The church has shown forgiveness and redemptive mercy.

But some of the greatest trophies of His grace that I am thinking about right now will never make it in the pages of

Christian books, or as the subject of articles in our Christian magazines. They won't become speakers at Christian bookseller conventions, or at Sunday school conventions, (though there are a few exceptions), because they are divorced and remarried. But you will find them faithfully serving on church boards, as trustees, deacons, elders, choir members, Sunday school teachers, and in other places of leadership responsibility, because their churches have decided to let God be the judge. They have followed in Jesus' steps, holding out arms of love, mercy, and grace—linking themselves with them in redemptive ways.

Dr. Ellisen states: "The blessing Jesus promised was to the 'pure in heart,' not necessarily the pure in history. It is through such individuals that He pours His blessing of redemptive grace, and we can ill afford to shut off any such channel through which God has chosen to work." He points to those whom God has redeemed and to their "reconstituted homes, the members of which are vibrant and thankful testimonies of that grace. To stifle that testimony at the church level smacks more of Pharisaism than of the redemptive grace and power of God. The command to serve is given to both redeemed individuals and redeemed homes."[8]

Many books have been written showing how to deal with guilt—real or imagined—and depression, feelings of failure. One book that has helped me tremendously is Erwin W. Lutzer's *Failure: The Back Door to Success*. I came to understand more fully that the potential for every sin lies within each of us, and if someone is free from guilt, it is because of God's grace, not because he or she is inherently better than others! There are a lot of Christians playing it safe, not divorcing, and the thing that is keeping them in line, so to speak, is the fear that this would ruin their reputations. They aren't considered failures in their marriages; but remember, God judges the heart; they are failures in their hearts. They are as guilty as if they had gone for a divorce decree. Lutzer says, "One molehill is nearly the height of another, if you measure them all against the Himalayas." The point is, the reason we think there are great differences between Christians is that we compare our lives, or the life of someone who is divorced and remarried, for instance, with those of other believers or those who haven't gone through that kind of trauma. Try comparing yourself or someone whom you greatly admire, or who is greatly admired and listened to, with God. But God, you see, judges righteously because He, and He only, takes everything into account. He knows what precipitated your divorce. Against the backdrop of God's holiness, we all come far short of God's standard.

In my own life, recognition of this helped clear the way for me to let go of the past and the guilt that cropped up whenever I was reminded of certain things. Furthermore, I began to realize that some people were really successful because they had lived a pretty normal life. That is, they've not had much chance to fail—things have gone well for them; they made a good marital choice, probably they were raised in a pretty normal kind of home with good role models. Some of us just struck out on many counts. I read books and see theologians in the pulpit, and in some instances, those saying things that put guilt on the backs of divorced and remarried people talk about their beautiful home lives—you know they've had great educations, and a lot of good breaks along the way. At times I've wanted to cry out, "God, it just isn't fair." But, of course, God knows; He knows what some of the rest of us have been through. And His word to us is, "Trust me."

Dr. Lutzer believes the greatest single cause of spiritual defeat is a guilty conscience. "We know we have sinned and are weary of it; yet we don't know how to be free from a sense of failure." He calls it a "futile cycle." How true! Discouragement sets in along with the guilt, and we feel like we've really blown it. Jim Elliot, martyred missionary to the Auca Indians, once said, "Discouragement is a satanic tool that seems to fit my disposition very well." Amen!

It was Lila Trotman, wife of Dawson Trotman (founder of The Navigators) whom the Lord used to help me gain an understanding of the devil's strategies. Lila was one of the "cameos" in my book, *Cameos: Women Fashioned by God.* One day she phoned me from Colorado just at the time I was struggling with discouragement, to say, "Helen, I don't exactly know why I'm calling you except God has impressed you upon my heart in such a strong way, I feel I must talk to you. I just want to remind you that you have an enemy, and he's a trained strategist. Read I Peter 5:8." How great it is when someone follows the promptings and nudging of the Holy Spirit. That day I read: "Be sober, be vigilant; because your adversary the devil, as a roaring lion, walketh about, seeking whom he may devour; whom resist stedfast in the faith" (I Pet. 5:8, 9a KJV). This, too, helped me to grasp as fact the reality that God has a "cure" for the guilt syndrome. With His help, I can now resist the feelings of guilt and discouragement over sin and failure that have been forgiven.

Dr. Lutzer explains that "The greatest blunder of Christians is not their failure when trying to live for Christ; a greater mistake is that they do not understand God's provision for sin, defeat, and guilt! We are successful to the extent that we understand God's remedy for failure." Here is how Dr. Lutzer explains "God's cure for the guilt syndrome" (paraphrased by myself):

1. Christ's death on the cross included a sacrifice for *all* our sins, past, present, and future (Col. 2:13).
Sometimes you will hear a Christian say, "It's hard to forgive . . ." and he or she will mention someone's name and something they've done.
Dr. Lutzer says, "God does not find it 'hard' to forgive us. It is not as though He must regretfully give us a second chance. The price of forgiveness has already been paid, and God wants us to accept it freely.
"Christ 'is the propitiation for our sins: and not for ours only, but also for the sins of the whole world' (I Jn. 2:2 KJV). That means He satisfied God for all sins which can *possibly be committed.*"
2. God cannot punish us for our sins! All of the punishment for sin has already been given to Christ (Isa. 53:10).

For that one agonizing over the death of a loved one, feeling that somehow he was responsible—that God was punishing him for his divorce and remarriage—Lutzer says God disciplines us, but He does not punish us. God's anger and justice for sin were satisfied at the cross. God isn't trying to get even with us when some calamity befalls us.

3. "Although we may become weary of confessing the same sins, God does not become weary of hearing our confession. If we say to God, 'I am coming to confess the same sin,' God's reply is, 'What sin?' Any previous sins which have been confessed *have already been blotted out* forever! 'I have wiped out your transgressions like a thick cloud,' God told His people (Isa. 44:22 NASB).

In a sense, by clinging to our guilt we are saying that we doubt the value of Christ's sacrifice. Sometimes the consequences of past sin remain, as Lutzer explains, "but the guilt (the legal condemnation for the offense) is gone.

"Our basis for pleasing God? Is it standing by faith on the sacrifice of Christ, a sacrifice which satisfied the Father completely. We are accepted *in the beloved!* And that basis remains secure even when we fail!"[9]

I am immensely grateful to Dr. Lutzer for his insights on failure and guilt and how to handle them. He points out that many Christians are "handcuffed by regret." We all can think of people who are plagued by the "If onlys," who nurse their regrets and cling to their grief and guilt. Why? It is an unconscious way of trying to pay for their sins or shortcomings, whatever. If you are tempted to live by "if onlys," think about this: "It is an insult to Christ if we believe His sacrifice was not enough for us!"[10]

It was Shakespeare who said, "What's done is done." It is true that in some respects our failures in the past may change or even curtail future ministry, but this same failure as it relates to the divorced and remarried can serve as a stepping-stone into a satisfying future.

As we deal with the "formerlies"—former spouse, former friends, former work, former church—making certain we have wiped the slate clean by asking forgiveness where needed, making restitution where necessary, and doing the thing that must be settled, we are clearing the way for potential in the present. It is a matter of housecleaning our attitudes to a large extent. Along with this is the matter of dropping our defenses; God isn't interested in our excuses, nor are our friends and family.

Finally, as we seek to walk on as divorced-remarried Christians, free from the stain of sin and guilt brought on by divorce, let us remember what it is that the Father really wants from us. Does he want primarily our service—whether it be as pastors, teachers, missionaries, or generous lay men and women—or is there something else that is more important? Perhaps your church has excluded you from the kind of service you feel you are best suited for now that you are divorced or divorced and remarried. You are hurting; you are questioning this. Or perhaps you are suffering along with someone who has been deprived of such service. Listen to Lutzer's wise counsel—counsel that has helped me immeasurably:

Consider the familiar verse, "But if we walk in the light as He Himself is in the light, we have fellowship with one another, and the blood of Jesus His Son cleanses us from all sin" (I John 1:7 NASB). This does not merely mean that if we walk in the light, we have fellowship with other Christians: it means that if we walk in the light, we have fellowship with God and He has fellowship with us! We and God have fellowship one with another.

We not only have the privilege of having fellowship with God, *but God desires to have fellowship with us!* He seeks our fellowship. He seeks our worship.

God is looking for worshipers. And if the religious elite are too proud or too busy to learn to worship Him, He seeks the worship of those whose lives are trapped in moral ruin. Perhaps they, like the woman of Samaria, can more readily appreciate God's forgiveness; perhaps they are better candidates for two-way fellowship with the Creator! The Father seeks such to worship Him.

Worship is possible even for those who are victims of an unhappy marriage or crushing emotional experiences. It's a possibility for us all.

Those who truly worship, truly serve. The Father seeks such to worship Him![11]

The next time the enemy sidetracks you and tries to get you off course by laying unnecessary guilt on you, stop, think, and ask yourself: Is this necessary?

Consciously place yourself once again in the hands of the Father, and walk on in the light. Then go a step further. If you have distanced yourself from a church that has disappointed you, disciplined you, or let you down in some way, continue to seek out a church that meets your needs and where you can worship the Father along with other believers. Such churches do exist. You need that, and you should know—the church needs what *you* have to offer.

Notes

1. Stanley A. Ellisen, *Divorce and Remarriage in the Church* (Grand Rapids: Zondervan, 1980), pp. 75, 76.

2. Ibid., p. 88.

3. Larry Richards, *Remarriage: A Healing Gift from God* (Waco, Tex.: Word Books, 1981), p. 85.

4. Ibid., pp. 85, 88.

5. Dwight Hervey Small, *The Right to Remarry* (Old Tappan, N.J.: Revell, 1975), p. 20.

6. Ibid., p. 184.

7. Ibid., p. 183.

8. Ellisen, p. 89.

9. Erwin W. Lutzer, *Failure: The Back Door to Success* (Chicago: Moody Press, 1975), summarized and paraphrased from chapter 5, "How Much Can God Forgive?"

10. Ibid., p. 60.

11. Ibid., pp. 104, 105.

Chapter Six

FORGIVENESS
The Great Biblical Ideal

One woman—a Christian author and speaker—while going through a divorce, received a letter in the mail containing three words: FORGIVEN BUT DISQUALIFIED. One is left to wonder what that letter-writer does with the sin and failure of the apostle Peter who denied Jesus three times. (The account is told in Matthew 26:69-74, and in Mark 14:66-72.) Did Jesus disqualify Peter for future discipleship?

We cannot think of divorce and remarriage without considering the meaning of Christian forgiveness.

R. Lofton Hudson, founding director of the Midwest Christian Counseling Center in Kansas City, Missouri, and the Center for Christian Counseling in Omaha, Nebraska, observes that if we were to follow Jesus in the understanding of forgiveness, we would say, "Go, and sin no more" (John 8:11 KJV).

THE TRULY CHRISTIAN APPROACH TO FAILURE

Dr. Hudson does not take the position that all divorced or divorced-remarried people should be presumed guilty of some kind of gross sin (which is quite often thought), but if our definition of sin is "missing the mark," then in that respect they may have sinned by missing the mark of perfection in marriage. Still, Dr. Hudson says:

We can hardly afford to judge and take one of the following attitudes: "You have made your bed hard, lie in it"; or "Limp the rest of your life—you are a cripple, a failure; God will forgive you but you will never get over it, so bear your cross bravely." The Christian approach to those involved in marriage failure, even when due to their fault, is: "Be thou made whole" and "If we confess our sins, he is just, and may be trusted to forgive our sins and cleanse us from every kind of wrong" (I John 1:8, NEB)—even lousing up a marriage.[1]

Dr. Hudson quotes William Barclay, renowned professor of New Testament at the University of Glasgow, who, after reviewing the climate in the world of Jesus and Paul, concerning the home and divorce, says, "There are other things than adultery which can kill a marriage and the love which should be in it."[2]

Dr. Barclay warns against turning the words of Jesus into law, thus forgetting that the greatest thing of all is love. He insists that if two people find living together an impossibility, they should take whatever help they may need from the minister, priest, psychologist, or psychiatrist. After they have taken that, and, "the situation is still beyond mending,"

Then I do not think that it is an act of Christian love to keep two such people tied together in a life of torture; nor do I think that it is right for them to be allowed to separate and never be allowed to try to start again. In such circumstances I believe that divorce is the action of Christian love, for I do not think that Jesus would have insisted that two utterly incompatible people should be condemned to drag out a loveless existence, heartbreaking for themselves and disastrous for their children. Nor do I believe that they should be forbidden to remarry and to remarry with the blessing of the church. Nor do I think I would wish to talk much about innocent and not innocent parties, for when a marriage breaks up I should doubt if there is any such thing as an altogether innocent and an altogether guilty party.[3]

Forgiveness. Love. You cannot have one without the other.

Dr. Hudson refers to a 1971 report put out by a commission appointed by the Archbishop of Canterbury in 1968, which sets forth the views of the Church of England. After a careful study of every passage pertaining to marriage and divorce, the commission concluded, concerning divorce, that "there are occasions when divorce could bring a blessed relief from intolerable conditions for both wife and children. . . . In an actual human situation . . . where marriage has already broken down, people have to go from where they are . . . when Jesus asserted the permanence of marriage, he did not thereby rule out of court the propriety of all divorce and remarriage."[4]

THE CONFUSED CHRISTIAN APPROACH

Many church people are unsure how to treat divorced and divorced-remarried people, as illustrated by some examples that have come to my attention. I have a heartbreaking letter from a young woman who had been dating for several months, in her words, "a super guy studying for the ministry." The relationship was getting more serious; both felt they loved the other, but then he told her he could not continue the relationship because "he had no peace about marrying a 'divorced woman.' "

This woman described her reactions to that in her letter to me: "That label, 'divorced woman,' is a killer. My emotions and whole being have been through so much. There have been questions, anxiety, guilt, fear, and depression scattered through the times of joy and peace and growth in the Lord."

She had been a Christian when she married and so was her husband. But during the years after her marriage, she came close to a mental collapse as she coped with "a horrifying marriage situation, and through much anguish and heartache, divorce became inevitable. Through it all, the Lord has drawn close to me. He has brought me safely through, and I have grown into a new person because of it."

One of the contributing factors in her spiritual growth is her loving parents and a wonderful, loving church family. But even though she experienced that love and acceptance, "Still, I have been confronted so many times with the stigma of divorce that I have felt as if a huge 'D' was burnt on my chest and clothing, and that's all that people can see about me. Things have been said to me by well-meaning Christians that have hurt down to the core of my heart. Some people just can't seem to find it in their hearts to grant forgiveness to the divorced person."

Added to that hurt, of course, was the final blow of the rejection by the man she had come to love—a Christian man studying for the ministry. One can only speculate on what might have happened if he had gone ahead and married her. The day might have come, indeed, when he would have had trouble finding a church that would accept a pastor married to a divorced woman.

But which is worse—the plight of this young woman or the situation described in another letter I received?

"I am finding myself confronted with the dilemma of whether to stay with a marriage that has caused me much psychological and emotional pain, or to venture into the unknown. . . . When I married my husband, I thought he had accepted Christ, but over the seventeen years of marriage I've not seen any of the fruit of the Spirit develop. I feel alone spiritually in this marriage, which can only be described as a constant battle. I have long felt compressed into some sort of impossible mold. . . . Long ago I lost respect for my husband. I lost all joy in being a wife and have felt very little, if any, kind of emotion for him at all. My husband starting calling me 'a dried-up old woman' (I was only twenty-eight then). . . .

"Much of this time our marriage was just hell. For a long while, I repressed everything deeply. Then I felt hatred for my husband. I got to the point where I couldn't even pray to God. . . . But God finally helped me deal with the resentment and the anger I was repressing, and He helped me forgive my husband for all the cruel things he'd said and done. So while I no longer resent him, I have no feelings of love left for him, either. I haven't been able to say 'I love you' for four years. I am living in limbo—not divorced, certainly not really married. We are separate beings, not united in marriage.

"I only have peace because I am committed to God and behaving myself. I do attend church. But there is a nothingness to our marriage and only tension within our home. My husband and I have practically nothing in common and our ways of thinking war against each other.

"Now I'm trying to decide what to do. Recently I told my husband I thought it was unfair to both of us to stay married because I seriously doubt that our feelings for each other will ever change. (Too much has happened.) I'm not saying God couldn't bring about these changes, but it doesn't appear that this is going to happen. We have four lovely children (all under age thirteen). I talked to two pastors, and all they could say was that it was God's will for us to stay married and that God could create love in each of us for the other. But both of them admitted they didn't know of any similar cases where love had been rekindled like that. I'm tired of being unhappy but frightened of being divorced. And, of course, I hate hurting the kids. . . ."

I have received other similar letters, and my husband and I have talked to many individuals, all of whom described the initial decision about whether to go through with a divorce as "an agonizing time in my life." As a divorceé this woman would have a tough time of it. Added to all the practical problems that would have to be worked out—getting a job, hiring a babysitter, supporting the children, fighting for custody, working through the loneliness and subsequent guilt, struggling with her religious background and conditioning (that divorce and remarriage are no-no's)—would be the inevitable fact that she would want to date other men, she would be hopeful about remarriage. But she has four children. Not many men are willing to take that on as a responsibility. So the fears expressed by this woman are legitimate fears. One of the most difficult things she would have to handle is the unforgiving attitude of many Christians.

WALKING WITH THOSE IN TROUBLE

I have always felt it was important in talking to individuals contemplating divorce, or in responding to those who had written me, to help them understand that remarriage isn't necessarily what they should be seeking or even hoping for on the other side of divorce. It was, therefore, interesting to hear from a woman who has been through two divorces, and who had read my book *The Other Side of Divorce* twice. Sue wrote:

> "One important thing God helped me to understand as a result of reading your book was that "the other side of divorce" isn't marriage, but rather it is reached by a walking-through process—to get to the other side requires action. If divorced people could only grasp the fact that another marriage isn't going to solve their problem, unless they have indeed gone through a healing."

Many individuals, like the woman who wrote the long letter, are paralyzed by fear. What primarily are their fears? Fear of the unknown, fear of the wrath of God, fear of what the church will say. What could the church do to help people in such desperate marital situations when counseling doesn't bring about the necessary changes to allow the couple to live in harmony? Surely one of the things the church could do is to take steps to allay their fears—to assure them of God's love, mercy, and forgiveness—to assure them that the church can practice godly forgiveness—that if, in fact, people do have to "walk through" a divorce, the church will walk through with them.

Sue and her husband taught a class of divorced individuals. Her letter continues:

> "Another idea got blown away during that class—time doesn't heal, no matter what people say—it just numbs. True healing can only come from the inside, through Jesus. . . . It's amazing how God allows us to help others from our own experiences—that's been part of the healing process. Someone's today is my yesterday; how good God is to allow our lives to touch that someone's!"

Yes, indeed, how good! The church can also help to hasten the healing process by extending the kind of forgiveness that says, "But for the grace of God, I would be in your shoes," and showing such hurting people that God sees not only the wickedness of sinners (those of us who fall short of God's perfection), but the weaknesses of His saints. Christ is Christianity's greatest credential. If we will but point hurting hearts in His direction and become walking demonstrations of His compassion, such fear can be transformed into dynamic faith—the kind of faith Sue and others who responded to the questionnaire demonstrate as they reach out to those who are struggling.

THE CHALLENGE TO THE CHURCH

From beginning to end, the Bible shows us God's mercy, forgiveness, and love. We must be people of the Book, and unforgiveness and an unredemptive attitude on the part of the church are not in keeping with the Bible's standards. The challenge to the church is (and always has been) to clearly and unhesitatingly teach biblical truth, but its mission is also to forgive sins (John 20:21-23) and to minister to the fallen. It surely must not condemn those whom the Bible does not condemn, and it must always be prepared to bind up the wounds of the brokenhearted, and to do what it can to restore to spiritual wholeness those whose lives have fallen apart because of their marriage breakups. God is always able to start with His children where they are. The forgiving love of the gospel as practiced by God's people can bring healing ministry to all who fall short of the biblical ideal.

One Sunday I was introduced to a woman who had been a former member of our church. In the course of our conversation, I made the mistake of asking her where she was now worshiping. She mentioned the church, and I recognized the pastor as being the author of a book I had just read on the subject of marriage, divorce, and remarriage.

"Oh yes," I told her. "I've just read your pastor's new book."

She picked up on it immediately. "Didn't you enjoy it? Isn't it wonderful?"

Being unwilling to lie, even to fudge a little when it comes to my opinion on books, I had to say that while he was a good

91

communicator, I didn't agree with many of his views, especially his views about divorce and remarriage.

"But it's *all* biblical," she stated very firmly.

"Yes . . . but it's not the *whole* counsel of God; the Bible has something to say also about God's mercy, love, and forgiveness," I countered.

With that she looked at me, turned on her heel, and walked away. Plainly, she was angry and disturbed at my reply. Among other things, this pastor-writer's counsel to divorced people is, "You must purpose not to remarry."

If anyone doubts that the forgiving love of the gospel practiced by God's people can help to bring healing to those who fall short of the biblical ideal, let them turn to II Corinthians 2:5-11. While this passage has some obscurities—we do not know what this man did to cause grief to Paul and the Christians in Corinth—what is clear is how Paul wanted the Christians to treat this man: "You ought to forgive and comfort him, so that he will not be overwhelmed by excessive sorrow. I urge you, therefore, to reaffirm your love for him" (II Cor. 7-8 NIV). The last verses speak of forgiveness. *The Living Bible* puts it: "He has been punished enough by your united disapproval. Now it is time to forgive him and comfort him. Otherwise he may become so bitter and discouraged that he won't be able to recover. Please show him now that you still do love him very much. . . . A further reason for forgiveness is to keep from being outsmarted by Satan; for we know what he is trying to do" (II Cor. 2:6-8, 11 TLB).

These are essential responses to the divorced and divorced-remarried in our midst: forgiveness, comfort, and reaffirmed love.

Notes

1. R. Lofton Hudson, *Lectures on Christian Theology* (DeLand, Fla.: Stetson Univ., February 2-4, 1977), p. 35.

2. As cited by Hudson. Quoted from William Barclay, *Ethics in a Permissive Society* (London: Collins Fontana Books, 1971), pp. 203-204. (Page 35 in Hudson's book.)

3. Ibid.

4. As cited by Hudson. Quoted from *Marriage, Divorce, and the Church* (London and Southampton: The Camelot Press, Ltd., 1971), pp. 94-95. (Page 33 in Hudson's book.)

I have quoted Dr. Hudson because I find his views compassionate, yet he upholds the biblical ideal without being rigidly legalistic. His research is complete, and he interprets the Bible according to the problems it addresses.

Chapter Seven

COMPASSIONATE THEOLOGY
Truth and Love

When it came time for me to consider remarriage, a well-meaning, perceptive psychologist friend said to me, "You came through the divorce pretty well—all things considered—but I must warn you that if you thought things were tough as you floundered in those chilly waters pretty much by yourself, you may well look back on the divorce experience as mild in comparison to the flak both of you will receive as divorced-remarried Christians."

Solemn words. I knew him well enough to undersand that he wasn't trying to talk me out of remarriage. He was trying to prepare me for what might lie ahead, and he knew what he was talking about.

NONCOMPASSIONATE THEOLOGY

The first place we encountered flak was from places where my husband sent resumés. After having spent much of his adult life in the womb of a Christian organization, my husband found himself without a job because of his divorce. As he tried to find employment in other Christian organizations, he received numerous turndowns. Each time he was asked if he had one of the biblical reasons for divorce. He was always open and honest, explaining the circumstances that convinced him he could no longer live a lie.

My husband was paying a price for his divorce and

remarriage. The fact that he had difficulty getting back into the Christian employment field was heartbreaking. What had happened? He was the same person that he had been before the divorce and remarriage. His job qualifications hadn't changed. At times he was tempted to wonder if God was extracting payment for his divorce and remarriage. But, of course, that is not the case; it is totally out of keeping with all biblical teaching on God's forgiveness and grace. This was and is a question other remarried Christians told us they wrestled with as well. The secular world could care less about your marital status, but the situation is far different in the Christian job arena. Dwight Small talks about this, describing it as "the evangelical *party line* on divorce and remarriage, better described as the *hard line*" (see p. 17 of Small's book); it is an "entrenched bias on this subject which characterizes much of evangelical Christianity" (see p. 16).

I know a dedicated Christian woman who was asked to leave a Southern California Christian college because she married a divorced man (who was in the ministry). Never mind that his wife left him and that he was not responsible for the divorce action. Never mind that he was the "innocent party." And never mind that she was close to graduation. How heartless and unforgiving can Christians get! Several years later it was discovered that on this same college campus scores of students were engaged in homosexual liasons, as well as some of the faculty members. The difference? These individuals were able to cover up their sins, while the "sin" of divorce and remarriage is an open failure on the part of two people. Christians don't know how to handle Jesus' words, spoken in absolute terms of prohibition and condemnation *to the Jewish people* who asked Him about divorce in the Matthew 19 passage, testing Him. These words are almost always lifted out of the context in which they were spoken—they are words that are in keeping with God's perfect, pure will. Seldom does the church interpret to her people that this must be clearly distinguished from situations in which God responds to human need, acting upon His mercy and grace, revealing His conditional will, as He accommodates Himself to the failures of His redeemed people.

I know the parents of a talented minister of music at a large church. This young man was asked to leave this church because he and his wife got a divorce and, after a couple of years, he was attracted to a woman in the singles' group and felt he'd like to strike up a friendship with her. When the relationship progressed to the serious stage—love developed, and he found he could love again—his position was wrested away from him. He had not instigated the divorce. He had not caused the rift in his first marriage. He was not consorting with another woman while married. The facts in this situation are painfully clear today, but they were equally clear at the time he lost his job. Today his former wife is married to the man she was secretly seeing while she was married to the young minister of music. The pain the parents of this fine son experienced was incredible—they shared it with me; I hope I was able to help them. I tried. Among other things, I told them I hoped their son would love again, that I knew God's redemptive grace included their son, and that I would pray that another church would extend a call to him, showing compassionate theology at work. And I'm happy to tell you that very thing did happen.

I know of a theologian who became the center of controversy in his denomination after he remarried. This was coupled with the sudden alienation from many of his ministerial friends. It seemed that his wife had died, and after a period of time, God graciously opened providential doors so that his path crossed that of a woman he had known long ago (in vacation Bible school and confirmation class days—so it had, indeed, been a long time). The problem arose because the woman was divorced. The theologian prayerfully and carefully thought on the matter of remarriage, but finally became fully convinced that God has no "second-class citizens" in His kingdom; "and . . . we may render difficulty to the biblical concept of His grace through an unwarranted interpretation of Holy Scripture." Among other persons, he pointed to C. S. Lewis, who married a divorced American poetess. He also pointed out that it is not a new departure to accept the view that remarriage of divorced persons could be within God's will, and that Saint Augustine changed his view and believed in divorce and remarriage. That same view was held by Luther, Calvin, Melanchthon, Wesley, and Spurgeon.

In this home, as in the homes of other remarried Christians, the Scriptures are read, Christ is honored, and prayers are offered, just as they are in homes where divorce and remarriage have not been experienced.

A friend of this gentleman told him that if he had married a prostitute who was coming off alcohol and drugs and had gotten converted, people would be asking him to bring her to their churches so they could hear her testimony. Instead, he married a fine Christian woman who had the misfortune to have gone through divorce, a woman who suffered a great deal of pain, but who "stayed by the stuff," rearing three children, and giving them Christian college educations. "But," his friend said, "I guess God's grace doesn't cover that!" This man resigned his position within the denomination after having served faithfully for more than twenty-eight years.

AMBIVALENT VIEWS OF CLERGY AND LAITY

Clearly, Christians are divided on this thorny issue. *Christian Life* magazine (January 1981) provided a forum for forty-five top evangelical Christian men and women to speak out on six important questions. The article, "Is There a Christian Point of View," asked "Is divorce and remarriage for the believer biblical?" There were seven yes answers, fifteen no's, and eight maybe's. In summation the article says:

Clearly, on this question panel members appeared to be more ambivalent than most. But the appearance is only surface. Using the Bible as their guide, the panelists agreed that it is difficult to distort Jesus' meaning when He said that divorce could be resorted to only in the case of adultery. The question of remarriage proved to be a little more difficult to handle. The consensus appeared to give the innocent party the freedom of choice. How to determine "who is innocent" panel members apparently felt had to be handled on an individualized basis.

97

Keith Miller, widely respected author, who is divorced and remarried, was on the panel voicing the view that would be endorsed by those of us who are among the divorced-remarried Christians in the nation. Miller says:

We should have integrity in our dealings with the world, and not be wishy-washy with regard to things we consider to be wrong. However, I keep looking at the way Jesus dealt with people like the prodigal son, the woman at the well, the woman caught in adultery. I believe strongly that we Christians should use Him as a model with regard to our dealings with people rather than pharisaically pronouncing judgment impersonally on the people and the questions they bring.

A similar view was expressed by Peter Gillquist, another author-friend and presiding bishop of the Evangelical Orthodox Church:

Lying is prohibited in the Law, yet Rahab was rewarded for her faithfulness. Romans 13 commands obedience to authorities, yet David didn't always, while Mary and Joseph took off to Egypt to avoid Herod's edict. . . . A pat "yes or no" is almost impossible.

Lest it seem that I am doing exactly what Keith Miller describes as showing pharisaical-like judgment, let me be quick to say that love is a two-way street. There can be no place for bitterness or cynicism by those of us who have been divorced and are remarried. We cannot indulge in that kind of attitude; it is crippling, emotionally draining, and we stand to be the losers. We must live by our convictions; you and I are not responsible for what another person chooses to believe or do, but we are responsible for our reaction. I can differ with you, but I must still love you.

I always have been opposed to generalizations. When Pete Gillquist said that a "pat 'yes or no' is almost impossible," he was surely alluding to the dangers inherent in generalizations. We are well advised to look at the whole counsel of the Lord as we act upon our convictions. In heaven we will not be able to attend the marriage feast of the Lamb by proxy. And in that eternal abode of those who have received God's forgiveness through Christ, we cannot be choosy about those with whom we will fellowship forever. Selective service may work today here on planet Earth as the Christian church and her leaders (and the Christian community) make their decisions affecting divorced and remarried Christians, but in heaven we may have to sit next to the woman Jesus encountered at the well. The possibility exists that those who have been refused here in the land of the living, and for whom all-embracing Christian love has been somewhat on the short side, may not find acceptance until they reach that blessed place where time shall be no more. Conservative Christian tradition may call for a strong stance against divorced-remarried individuals here, but you and I are not called to be the judges for those who hold to their beliefs. To love them in the here and now, and to leave all judging to God, is the only wise and safe course.

THE FLAK

As I stood alongside my husband after my remarriage, I remembered only too well my own struggle in the days following my divorce. I have already related how I became convinced of the need to hold out forgiveness to those who could not find it in their hearts to respond to me with understanding. Now once again I was being called on to practice these principles. I, too, found myself under fire as a result of remarriage. A major contract was broken by one publisher; other publishers stopped pursuing me for books. To this day, one publisher won't speak to me. I experienced bewilderment and pain when an author-friend at a convention came down the aisle toward me and deliberately turned her head and looked the other way. At a writer's conference where I was speaking, a writer-friend got up as I was being introduced and walked out of the room. Another friend had told me I was committing "career suicide." My reaction to that (not to her, but in my own thinking) was that "career murder" would have been more accurate—who was killing what? God hadn't removed the gift and love of writing. In fact, I found myself wanting to write and express myself in words on paper with a greater freedom than I'd ever known before. There were times when it was almost funny—some of the things that happened—except for the jagged, sharp, inner hurt.

AFFIRMATION AND COMPASSION

Finally, my husband secured a job interview. Once again he was open and honest and, to our joy, he was hired. We were so grateful. We knew God was doing something special. The job meant that we had to leave southern California, but we looked upon that as a blessing—we could start out afresh. Our reputations had preceded us—his because he had sung for years with the Haven of Rest quartet as lead tenor and soloist, mine because I was an author.

Some months after being on his new job, one of the Christian school board advisors (where my husband was the principal) came to us and said, "Someone has been making some ugly statements about you, and they have reached the school board's ears, but we want you to know we have been watching your life and your consistent witness. My wife and I, and the school board, refuse to believe these statements. We are convinced that God is honoring your work among us, and that He is blessing you."

That affirmation by the Reverend Rex Lindquist of Salinas, California, did something for us in the early days of our marriage. It reaffirmed our faith in God's people and made us realize that these people were representative of a *vast* number of Christians who, while upholding the teachings of the church and the sure Word of Scripture, still recognized that they could reach out compassionately to those who have gone through divorce and were now remarried.

The sensitivity of these good people in that community helped us realize that as long as we kept our eyes on the Lord, aware that He had forgiven us for past failures, we needn't fear the future. There was a balanced tension in what these people had done—they both upheld the truth and at the same time, they reached out in love. They did not allow themselves to be polarized in their struggle between truth and love.

This is a very Christian way of living. Jesus Himself

arbitrated against the legalism of His day. On one Sabbath day, Jesus and His disciples walked through wheat fields, and the disciples picked some of the wheat kernels to eat. The Pharisees were quick to challenge Jesus, saying His disciples had worked on the Sabbath. What was Jesus' answer? He reminded them about the time King David and his companions were hungry, and "he went into the house of God . . . and they ate the special bread only priests were allowed to eat" (Mark 2:25-26 TLB).

Jesus pointed out that this was against the law too. Then He went on to say, "But the Sabbath was made to benefit man, and not man to benefit the Sabbath. And I, the Messiah, have authority even to decide what men can do on Sabbath days!" (vv. 27,28 TLB).

If David, incidentally, had actually been convicted for doing what he did, the Jewish law said the death penalty should be inflicted. In this instance, back in Old Testament times, the preservation of David's life was far more important than preserving the bread! Jesus was making the point that people are more important than rules and rituals.

Jesus vividly demonstrated this attitude toward the woman taken in adultery and to her accusers. He deliberately set aside the letter of the law in this instance—by which law He Himself could have picked up the first stone to hurl at her, especially since He was without sin. But He was more concerned that He fulfill the law and save her. Here we see that the higher law of love saved an individual. Once again I turn to Dwight Small and his brilliant, compassionate analysis of this event in the life of our Lord:

A familiar situation greets us, for the first thing we read is: "And the scribes and the Pharisees brought a woman caught in adultery. . . . 'Now in the Law Moses commanded us to stone such women; what then do You say?' " (John 8:3-5 NASB). Once again Jesus is put to the test and made to interpret the law of Moses. Little did these Pharisees realize that He was the very Author of the law, and its final interpreter.

The important observation to be made first is that here we have an actual encounter of Jesus with a case of proven adultery. The context is that of the Mosaic Law and the challenge of the Pharisees as to Jesus' true relation to it. As verse 6 clearly states, "And they were saying this, testing Him, in order that they might have grounds for accusing Him. . . ." And what is remarkable is that Jesus, in no sense opposed to the law and given no teaching that would supersede it (such as in the Sermon on the Mount), gave them a direction which actually seemed to countenance the harsh penalty of the Mosaic Law. Yet the Lord of all grace was above the law which He had given, and the condition which He placed upon those who would execute the law changed everything. ". . . He who is without sin among you, let him be the first to throw a stone at her" (v. 7 NASB). We learn nothing new as to how Jesus regards the seriousness of adultery, for His law is absolute and uncompromised. What we do learn is how Jesus' response to failure is conditioned by grace. So what Jesus *does* stands in contrast with what Jesus *says*. And this is not of the nature of contradiction; it is the superseding nature of grace in the employment of the law's Author. And more than anything else this introduces us to the transition Jesus was even then making from the law, under which He had come, to the grace which was to rule in the Church Age.[1]

These self-proclaimed would-be executors of morality one by one slouched away. They could not carry out the condemnation of the law; they, too, were guilty of sin. The Sinless One released the woman from the penalty with His words of forgiveness as He dealt with her in grace. As Small points out, "Without compromising the law, Jesus nonetheless was completely redemptive: *there was no executed penalty!*"[2] And if these self-righteous Pharisees could not carry out the letter of the law, how dare we, as Christians under grace, presume that we are in so much better a position than they. Moreover, and of even *greater* significance, how dare we exemplify less grace and mercy than Jesus!

"Blessed are the merciful," said Jesus in His Sermon on the Mount (Matt. 5:7 KJV). And His commandment to us is, "Be ye therefore merciful, as your Father also is merciful (Luke 6:36 KJV).

The Catholic church has long struggled with divorce and remarriage. At one time their views were more rigid and inflexible than they are today. I am impressed with the compassionate stance taken by the North American Conference of Separated and Divorced Catholics (NACSDC). The Reverend James J. Young, NACSDC chaplain, and Sister

Paul Ripple, NACSDC executive director, have been in the forefront of that movement.[3] In one publication, they point their readers to an exhortation of Pope Paul VI in which he asked the church to be at once and the same time "servants of the truth" and "animated by love." It is a papal approach that is in harmony with the views of those Protestants and Protestant clergy and theologians who understand the example of Jesus and His dealings with people as He viewed and applied the law.

Catholics, however, still struggle especially with remarriage. An annulment—virtually a canceling out of a marriage—is the only way a Catholic may remarry and retain the privileges of the Catholic church. The church began recognizing psychological grounds as reason for an annulment in 1970, and it became church law in 1983.[4]

The church in general can do many things within the framework of upholding the truth and being loving toward those in need. George W. Peters, a professor of missions at Dallas Theological Seminary, has made the observation that while the church is a church militant, it may also need to become a salvation army, a home, a nursery, a hospital, a mending institute. "Let us make room in our churches for every repentant and forgiven sinner regardless of the past. There was room in the churches Paul founded."[5]

LOVE IN ACTION

My husband and I were recipients of this kind of love from the First Baptist Church of Salinas, California. We will never forget the welcome we received at the outset from the pastor and later from the church members. We had phoned for an appointment to meet the pastor on a Saturday afternoon. My husband explained that we were divorced and recently had married and were seeking a church home. (We would not force ourselves on any church in that community; we wanted an opportunity to explain our past to him.) We first met the Reverend Fred Fels outside the church. This magnificent man walked toward us with outstretched arms. I mean, his arms were spread as wide as they could possibly be. I shall never forget the impact of seeing him that way and the beauty in that embrace as he enfolded both of us in those arms. He was the personification of Jesus that day. This was the caring Jesus as love in action.

We grew spiritually in that church, surrounded by love and solid Bible teaching, and the friendships we made there have endured. How much we needed what those people provided! But how different it might have been, and I shudder to think what might have happened to us at that important time in our lives. Even though we both had been Christians for years, anything but love and acceptance at that juncture might have engendered a bitter spirit within us. We've seen it happen to others who have not received that kind of compassion.

Larry Richards (mentioned in chapters 4 and 5) explains that when we emphasize law and not grace because of our fears, we show a complete misunderstanding of the way God works to make realization of His ideal possible for His children. The reason it is so difficult for us to understand grace or to live it is that it goes against our perceptions of ourselves. "When threat is removed, we're afraid the old in us will burst out and do its worst. We would rather rely on rules to bar us from evil than on love to guide us to good."[6] It is this misunderstanding of grace and compassion that we see reflected in today's fears about divorce and remarriage.

"If we remove the threat of law," Richards explains, the feeling is, "then every married person will immediately run out and get a divorce, and remarry the first person he sees!"[7] (Well, probably not quite the *first* person, but what Richards is saying is that by letting down the legal restraints and adopting the concept of compassionate theology, the church will be, in a sense, encouraging divorce and remarriage.) Does Richards believe this is what most Christians would do? Do I believe that? Absolutely not! Retreat to law is, in a sense, a denial of grace. Instead, we are to trust each other to want to respond to God, to live up to His ideal as much as possible. Richards says, and I agree, that the Christian doesn't run out to divorce, because he loves God and wants to please him.[8]

So the fear in the church among Christians is that if we

accept remarriage as legitimate, everyone will hurry to get a divorce! "The fear is understandable. And the desire to uphold and strengthen marriage is commendable. But in our fear we may close our hearts to people . . . with deep hurts and needs."[9]

Grace is to operate in the world of realities where it can work its miracles in the real world of hardened human hearts. We need to pause at this point and repeat some of those words concerning grace:

For it is by grace you have been saved, through faith—and this not from yourselves, it is the gift of God—not by works, so that no one can boast (Eph. 2:8, 9 NIV).

For we do not have a high priest who is unable to sympathize with our weaknesses, but we have one who has been tempted in every way, just as we are—yet was without sin. Let us then approach the throne of grace with confidence, so that we may receive mercy and find grace to help us in our time of need (Heb. 4:15, 16 NIV).

But now a righteousness from God, apart from law, has been made known. . . . This righteousness from God comes through faith in Jesus Christ to all who believe. . . . for all have sinned and fall short of the glory of God, and are justified freely by his grace through the redemption that came by Christ Jesus (Rom. 3:21-23 NIV).

What is grace? It is God's favor that we don't deserve; we can't obtain it through our own striving—it is His gift. God's way of dealing with us should prompt us to be as loving. In the world of realities, this means surrounding the divorced and remarried in our midst with a caring, understanding community of concerned, loving people. This means helping them find redemptive ways to live through their experiences and to come out with as few scars as possible.

By upholding truth while holding out love, churches are saying that they will not compound the trauma of divorced and remarried people by indifference or hostility. They are saying they will respect the personal integrity of those who have gone through this experience, that the status of such individuals will not negate the church's love for them. With the help of the church, the divorce transition and remarriage can become a time of personal growth where the worth of the individual is affirmed.

How? In the generous and forgiving spirit of the God who loves us with His steadfast love.

Notes

1. Small, pp. 179, 180.
2. Ibid., p. 181.
3. For more information, write NACSDC, 5 Park Street, Boston, Mass. 02108.
4. Joe Zwack, an Iowa attorney, made himself an expert when he found he could not answer basic questions on annulment posed by Catholic clients in divorce cases. He researched Catholic canon law and wrote *Annulment: Your Chance to Remarry Within the Catholic Church* (New York: Harper & Row, 1983). Zwack tells Catholics that "there's a potential for almost any marriage that ends in divorce to be annulled" under looser guidelines adopted in recent years by the Catholic church in the United States. "The Church has made its position clear, and most Catholics are still in the dark on this," Zwack says, noting that the church does not want to be perceived as promoting the breakup of families.

It is sad that the church feels it has to resort to this means—annulment—and that they cannot go a step further and take to heart the exhortation of Pope Paul VI and truly be "servants of truth animated by love." Still, the acceptance of psychological grounds of divorce and remarriage does give those Catholics struggling with marriage mistakes and marriage problems a better chance than they had before.
5. Peters, p. 44.
6. Richards, p. 58.
7. Ibid.
8. Ibid.
9. Ibid., p. 20.

Divorce,
Remarriage,
and the
Individual

Chapter Eight

DESPAIR AND SUICIDE
An Eclipse in My Soul

I was tired beyond the telling, both physically and mentally. Every fiber of my being ached; nerves were taut; pressure had mounted to the exploding point; and depression had settled in like a heavy blanketing fog. My vision was obscured by the black pessimism of despair, and the future stretched before me as one long bout with loneliness. All I could see was work, loneliness, more work, and more lonely difficult hours of struggle. Work, loneliness, tiredness—the thoughts cycled through my mind in ceaseless repetition. Friends tried to be understanding, but I had the feeling that no one really understood what I was going through.

Earlier that week I had put my young son on the plane to spend the summer with his married sister in Canada. I was a divorced working woman. It seemed the better part of sense to have my son with his sister out on the ranch near Calgary rather than home alone while I was gone all day. I knew he would be well cared for, that there would be both work and play, that he could learn things about nature and life in that kind of an atmosphere that he could never learn in the city. Now it was Friday. The long weekend stretched ahead of me as I manuevered my car through the busy going-home-from-work traffic. Usually I, like other working men and women, welcomed the weekend, but on this June night, I was not anxious to get home. Another weekend in social exile was not what I needed. *What was there at home? Christy,* my beautiful and affectionate German shepherd. *What else?* I was talking to myself. *Work.*

A CRY FOR HELP

Work. I'd been working all week. Suddenly, I realized how depressing the thought of heading home to my typewriter was. *Oh, dear God, I can't stand much more of this,* I cried out in despair. But there it was, my gray shingled Cape Cod with the white picket fence, and Christy was greeting me—barking, jumping, wagging her tail, as I climbed out of the car. I was home.

I fed Christy, gave her fresh water, stooped to love and pet her absentmindedly, walked to the mailbox, methodically sorted, opened, and read some letters at the kitchen table, made my way through the house and sat down in my swivel chair in front of the typewriter. Suddenly, my head was on the typewriter, and I heard deep, groaning sounds. Sobs and sounds coming from somewhere. And then I realized once again how all alone I was. Those noises were from myself.

I've got to get out of here. I know, I'll go to Fullerton. Ed and Thelma will be home. I needed to be with people who knew me, who cared and understood about the struggle I was having in adjusting to the single life. In the back of my mind hovered the knowledge that God understood. He cared. He comprehended. But I was so weary of it all. I had no doubt about the reality of God, but at that point I needed someone with a face on. I needed God reaching out to me with human hands and human words and human love. I wanted a shoulder to lean on, someone else to help me carry the load besides God.

I drove thirty-five miles from my home under a mammoth weight of despair. Arriving at my destination, I literally jumped out of the car and ran up the sidewalk to my friends' front door. I rang the doorbell repeatedly, despair mounting. Deep inside I had known all along that they wouldn't be there—I hadn't called because I couldn't bear just the sound of a ringing telephone with no one there to answer. Now all I heard was the sound of the ringing doorbell. I don't recall the walk back to the car. But once again I was driving. Aimlessly. I was back in the community where my ex-husband and I had lived for a dozen or so years, but I couldn't think of a single place to go where I would be warmly welcomed.

It had been more than two years since I had walked out of my friends' lives, away from our church, away from two Christian bookstores that I had helped co-found and co-manage for nineteen years. I had decided that I would get the divorce with as little fanfare as possible. I would keep the disruption in other people's lives as a result of my action to a minimum by getting a job and moving away. But the void left in my life had been incredible. How difficult it was. How lonely. For the most part, two friends and their husbands stood with me. There might have been others who wanted to, but I was the one who made the choice not to encourage ongoing relationships. Now when I needed them so desperately, I didn't know where to turn. Instead, I drove slowly to the market, picked up a few groceries, then walked into the drugstore and had a prescription filled for sleeping pills.

I'd been having trouble turning my mind off at night—I'd work all day, come home at night, and write for hours on end. Then I'd fall onto the bed—perhaps collapse would be more accurate—and find myself unable to fall asleep. The doctor prescribed sleeping pills.

I drove slowly up and down the streets, past a couple of homes we had owned, trying to think what I could do, where I could go. At any point I could have stopped, could have walked up the walk to a former neighbor's door, and would have been welcome. But I didn't want to intrude into their lives. Small talk was not what I needed. I did need someone to hold me close, to tell me that this, too, would pass, that I could come out a survivor. Instead, I stopped the car in the park, reached into the glove compartment, and took out the unopened bottle of sleeping pills. There was a can of cola in the grocery bag. I opened it. My last thought was an anguished prayer: "God, forgive me, but I'd rather be with You."

Twelve hours later I awoke in my own bed. Was it a bad dream? A nightmare? No, I was fully clothed and in my hand was the bottle of sleeping pills, an empty bottle! A failed suicide!

"A WALKING MIRACLE"

I was now a statistic—a living statistic, to be sure. And I was not sure I was happy about it. "You are a walking miracle," the doctor later declared. "The pills should have done it, and if they hadn't, the thirty-five-mile drive back to your home certainly should have taken care of your desire to end it all. I don't understand how you drove that car back. If I never believed in angels before, I do now. Your guardian angel worked overtime! I have a feeling someone up there wants you around alive awhile longer."

For myself, at the time of the crisis in my soul, I needed someone to talk to. I had gone through the experience of divorce and had begun dating—always a strange experience and adjustment after you have lived in the world of the married. A relationship I had thought was going someplace came to an abrupt end when the gentleman was informed he had to make a choice—either stop seeing me or lose his job. The problem? I was a divorcée without one of the three accepted reasons for divorce in the Christian college where he was on staff.

I buried myself in my work. Though I attended church, I kept my defenses up. I couldn't risk being hurt again, and so I didn't become involved. I didn't attend the singles' classes or get-togethers. I made a feeble attempt at one church to participate but was so thoroughly disillusioned I gave up. Sometimes on Sunday mornings, I found it easier to stay at home and write than make the effort to go alone. (My son spent the weekends with his father for the most part.) Actually, my light of faith was flickering more often than glowing brightly.

FROM THE SHADOW OF SUICIDE

J. Wallace Hamilton, an imaginative, compassionate preacher, used to say, "If you want to believe, you have to stand where the light is shining."[1] If you want faith, go where others have found it, and expose yourself with some measure of regularity to the contagion of other people's faith. This means that you do not absent yourself from fellowshiping with other believers. This means that you go to the light of the Word. Hamilton calls the apostle Thomas, one of the disciples, the spiritual ancestor of the absentee—the man who wasn't there, the patron saint of a whole generation of Thomases living in a fog, wanting more faith. Why? Because, for whatever reason, they have detached themselves from Christian fellowship, the community of Christians who can be walking love and the human means God so often chooses to help us in our pilgrimage.

Thomas was not with Jesus' other disciples that night in the upper room when Jesus presented Himself to them. This was after Jesus' crucifixion, after His bodily resurrection (see John 20:19-29). But we're at fault when, like Thomas, we stand in our own light, when we won't come to where the light is, or when we won't expose our minds to the light.

How do we move from faithlessness, like Thomas, to faith? From the shadows of suicide to the light?

I didn't intend to write this chapter. But while I was working on the book, one Saturday morning we received a call and shortly thereafter a caller. Jim was very despondent and suicidal. My husband and I talked to him a long while. Jim had become a church bum, roaming from church to church, trying to find a place where he felt accepted. He was divorced, living in the shadows of dark despondency, spending too much time brooding in lonely solitude, burying his despair in hopelessness.

I told Jim that I had moved from suicidal despair to strong faith when I immersed myself once again in the Bible. It was the psalmist who became my companion as I went through this eclipse in my soul. Perhaps you are thinking: Strange, you shake your fist, as it were, in the face of God and try to do away with yourself, and then you retreat into the Bible. Strange perhaps, but true. I discovered that David, who wrote many of the psalms, had his highs and lows. In the crucible of daily living, David soared to heights of joy, and plummeted to the depths of despair. In his pilgrimage from doubt to certainty, in his conquest of despair, he laid bare his heart. I sought refuge and found the help I needed to sustain me through the difficult hours. The gamut of human experiences are reflected in those psalms—anguish and guilt, gloom and apprehension, fear, pain, grief, sadness, and weariness—all this and much more spoke to my aching heart. In my copy of *The Living Bible,* the book of Psalms is underlined and circled; there are exclamation points and little notes, all a solemn reminder, even today, that God had seen me and taken me through this crisis in my soul.

Some of those underlined excerpts read like this:

"Death bound me with chains, and the floods of ungodliness mounted a massive attack against me. Trapped and helpless, I struggled against the ropes that drew me on to death.

"In my distress I screamed to the Lord for his help. And he heard me from heaven, my cry reached his ears. . . . he sped swiftly to my aid. . . . Suddenly the brilliance of his presence broke through the clouds. . . .

"He reached down from heaven and took me and drew me out of my great trials. He rescued me from deep waters. He delivered me. . . .

"The Lord held me steady. He led me to a place of safety, for he delights in me" (Ps. 18:4-6, 12*a*, 16, 17*a*, 18*b*, 19 TLB).

I remember stopping in my reading when I read, *"He delights in me."* Was it really true? *Me?* I knew the Bible was a timeless book; its very timelessness made it applicable to every age of history. So it did include *me.* I read on.

"You have turned on my light! The Lord my God has made my darkness turn to light. Now in your strength I can scale any wall, attack any troop.

"What a God he is! How perfect in every way! All his promises prove true. He is a shield for everyone who hides behind him. For who is God except our Lord? Who but he is as a rock?" (Ps. 18:28-31 TLB).

Oh, how I needed a strong rock to lean against. There followed long periods of anguish when I would pour out my heart to the God the psalmist said cares for me in my distress—to the God "Who is merciful."

"Lord! Help!"

"Lord, lead me as you promised me you would. . . . Tell me clearly what to do, which way to turn."

God was at work directing my turning. It was difficult. I told Jim that I knew you don't just jump up from "trying to go sideways" (a term for suicide) and immediately walk a straight, steady line. I limped, struggled, stumbled, and cried. Sometimes I fell down. Then again I would cry out like David.

"Pity me, O Lord, for I am weak. Heal me, for my body is sick, and I am upset and disturbed. My mind is filled with apprehension and gloom. Oh, restore me soon.

"Every night my pillow is wet with tears . . . I am depending on you, O Lord my God" (Ps. 6:2-3, 6*b*, 7 TLB).

It was not a misplaced dependence. God could be depended upon to heal the hurting me.

"Mark this well: The Lord has set apart the redeemed for himself. Therefore he will listen to me and answer when I call to him. Stand before the Lord in awe, and do not sin against him. Lie quietly upon your bed in silent meditation. Put your trust in the Lord, and offer him pleasing sacrifices.

"Many say that God will never help us. Prove them wrong, O Lord, by letting the light of your face shine down upon us. . . . I will lie down in peace and sleep, for though I am alone, O Lord, you will keep me safe" (Ps. 4:3-6, 8 TLB).

From one who has been there, you can take it as truth: He is a God who helps; He is a God who can be trusted; and He is a God who keeps His children safe. When we are alone, as so many are, He is a reality.

GOD UNDERSTANDS

I made many discoveries in those days coming up out of the pit of despair. The psalmist's mood in the Bible so often fit mine. He reflected my own spirit. There was release from my own deep inner hurt as I, with the writer, laid my wounded spirit at the feet of Jesus.

I had been saved from myself. I began slowly to see that I was my own worst enemy—that in giving way to self-pity, and surrendering to black moods of oppression, I was shutting myself away from the love and help I so desperately craved. I needed to take myself in hand *and then hand myself over to God.* At that time, I remember saying, "Dear God, You are really getting the short end of this deal. I'm no bargain. . . ." Believe me, I found out that God doesn't mind!

In the Psalms I discovered that God was my shield who would defend me, that He is a judge who is perfectly fair. Over and over again the psalmist told me that God is good, *so good.* David said to this God of goodness, "I cannot understand how you can bother with mere puny man, to pay any attention to him!" (Ps. 8:4 TLB). That same thought frequently crossed my mind. Out of the fullness of his heart, David exclaimed, "O Lord, I will praise you with all my heart, and tell everyone about the marvelous things you do. I will be glad, yes, filled with joy because of you. . . . you have vindicated me, you have endorsed my work, declaring from your throne that it is good" (Ps. 9:1-2, 4 TLB).

And to think that I had thought I needed someone else to help me carry the load besides God! Shame engulfed me, remorse for my foolish act.

"All who are oppressed may come to Him. He is a refuge for them in their times of trouble. All those who know your mercy, Lord, will count on you for help. For you have never yet forsaken those who trust in you" (Ps. 9:9-10 TLB).

"Tell the world about his unforgettable deeds" (Ps. 9:11*b* TLB).

I was a writer. I read that and the thought flashed across my mind: *God, are You trying to get a message across to me? You mean, God, You aren't through with me? You mean I can still write and that someone will still publish for me?*

In my ears I was hearing someone tell me, "You'll never be published again. . . ." Now those words were becoming just a dim echo.

When David wrote that he felt helpless, overwhelmed, and in deep distress, and that his problems seemed to go from bad to worse (Ps. 25:16), I, as a woman, alone, making the adjustment to a new job in a strange community, having been rejected by someone I greatly admired, could feel some of the guilt about my own suicide attempt slip away. Here was "a man after God's own heart" making that kind of confession.

"See my sorrows; feel my pain; forgive my sins. . . . Save me from them! Deliver [me] from their power! Oh, let it never be said that I trusted you in vain!

"Assign me Godliness and Integrity as my bodyguards, for I expect you to protect me and to ransom [me] from all [my] troubles" (Ps. 25:18, 20-22 TLB).

In my mind's eye, I could see David lifting his hands to heaven imploring God's help. And just as God didn't ignore David's cry, I knew He would help me, too. David, to our knowledge, did not make an attempt on his own life, but you get the feeling that he must have felt like it many times.

As my husband and I talked with our friend Jim, we were able to help him understand that the thing missing in his life was *hope*. We understood that life had lost its meaning, that the situation in which he found himself appeared hopeless. I told him that I had come to understand that death by suicide was an emergency exit, which I felt would free me from facing the immediate present and the inevitable tomorrow with its pain and problems. But man-sized problems require God-sized solutions. "Go to the top for help, Jim. . . ."

HOW TO ESCAPE FROM DESPAIR

Out of all of this in that lonely summer of 1972, I came to understand several things. *First, I recognized once again who my enemy was.* The devil, our sworn enemy, is a "murderer from the beginning" according to John's gospel (John 8:44 KJV). The devil is happiest when he destroys one of God's children.

Second, the resources at our disposal are adequate for any and all our needs. God, the Creator of the universe, is big enough to create and take care of the world and still be interested in you and me as individuals. Jesus knows our souls in adversity. He knows every question, every doubt that plagues our thoughts. Every wound that inwardly bleeds is known to Him. The psalmist knew that. He said, "He that keepeth thee will not slumber. Behold, . . . he shall neither slumber nor sleep" (Ps. 121:3*b*-4 KJV).

If you are contemplating suicide, wishing to escape the world with its problems and difficult people, Jesus speaks those words to you also. It is as if He is saying, "If you have invited me into your heart, then let your mind rest on that, even though circumstances around you are disturbing and upsetting." His words are meant to convey the idea that you are not to be in a state of confusion or hurry. Rest on Him. Be sensible. Patient. Keep possession of your soul and your mind, even though you can't keep anything else. Grasp hold of the reality of God and don't let go. It is this that will energize and fortify you against every onslaught of Satan, who would seek to destroy you and rob you of your faith. Struggle can only make you more patient, sensitive, and godlike, when through God's strength and power, you overcome it.

Remember Job? Everything that meant anything to him had been destroyed, swept away, demolished—even his children. But can't you see him lifting his boil-covered arm to heaven and shouting, "Though he slay me, yet will I trust in him" (Job 13:15*a* KJV).

Third, stop looking for God to wave some magical wand that will give you all the answers to your questions and remove all the obstacles and problems. Intead, *act on your faith,* weak as it may be, and then watch God move in response to your first feeble steps for Him. Your destiny is terribly important to God.

I'm a very practical person. I realized that if things were going to get better it would have to begin with me. I couldn't wait around and expect others to do for me what I had to do for myself. (I've always liked Nehemiah. What a man! When confronted with the raw realities of his situation, he intensified his prayers, but then he set up a guard against his enemies. Great guy! He was the opposite of the old saying, "He is so heavenly minded, he's no earthly good.") I analyzed my situation and took decisive practical action. I prayed for wisdom and good common sense. The Lord provided both and, in time, my efforts paid off.

Sometimes criticism doesn't die down—it intensifies. Charles Swindoll explains that some people shrink to the size of their critics, trying to right every alleged wrong, to answer every accusation. In so doing, they become petty pygmies. That's enervating. I decided I would let God vindicate me; I didn't have the energy to waste on doing that and, besides, I didn't need to. The Bible is clear on that point. There are basically only two ways to fight: one is on your knees, the other is on your feet. I spent a lot of time on my knees. But then I did the near-at-hand things, keeping my writing commitments, fulfilling my contracts, thankful that God had supplied this means of supporting myself. It was a case of productive activity coupled with accepting the challenge of change, all the while trusting God to move on my behalf—not because I was so deserving, but because I knew He was faithful. I remembered that one time one of my children asked me if God was magic and I had told her no, but He was fair and faithful, all-seeing and all-knowing, which is a lot better than magic.

Fourth, we need to be thankful. I've already mentioned this and our need to praise God for who He is. In the midst of praise, Satan is rendered helpless. Our problems persist as long as we bask in them, feeling sorry for ourselves, all turned inward, failing to recognize that God is still taking care of us, that He wants to help us. In Psalm 56, David complains of his enemies—then with a resounding note of triumph, he declares emphatically, "This one thing *I know: God is for me!* I am trusting God—oh, praise his promises!" (Ps. 56:9*b*, 10 TLB).

Then David adds, "Thank you for your help. For you have saved me from death and my feet from slipping, so that I can walk before the Lord in the land of the living" (vv. 12*b*, 13 TLB).

What we are feeling when we are so lonely, physically tired, and emotionally depleted is but an expression of what we have always sought after—reality. We want something definite, something tangible. In our "wanting," we neglect to thank God for His unseen Presence.

Fifth, seek fellowship and help from the church and Christians. If you don't find such help, then don't give up on God; look elsewhere until you find Christians with whom you can relate. Go a step further; offer yourself to others who are hurting; in the doing, you will find your own hurt and loneliness abating. You will make the amazing discovery that life can be strong and rich and full of meaning in direct proportion to your willingness to release your capacity to love on the world. Remember, we are to be walking love to each other.

If you have walked away from former friends, now is the time to walk back into their lives. Confess your failures; ask for forgiveness. Humble yourself and see what God does. Make the necessary overtures; if you are rejected, then say to yourself, even as I learned to do, "Well, that's their problem; I know I've done the right thing," and get on with living.

Sixth, take charge of your health. Take care of yourself physically, I had overextended myself. Often when you live alone, you fail to eat properly; you may not get enough rest or exercise. Get as much rest as you can. Good sound sleep is therapeutic.

You may remember that at the beginning of this chapter I described my physical and mental condition at the time of my suicide attempt. The two were closely related. When you are down physically, you are down mentally and emotionally. Many people are borderline, if not actual, hypoglycemic. This means they have low blood sugar, a much misunderstood health problem. Physical problems have psychological manifestations that can lead to irrational behavior, emotional instability, distorted judgment, and nasty personality defects.

Learn to listen to the signals your body sends you. There is much you can do to help yourself; the challenge is interesting, even exciting as you see your body responding. I am especially grateful to Gladys Lindberg, founder of and nutrition consultant for Lindberg Nutrition Service in Southern California. She is a remarkable woman who has taught me much about the essentials of good health maintenance. Her book, *Take Charge of Your Health,*[2] is a gold mine of information. It has become my "health Bible."

The seventh thing I strongly recommend is to give in to your emotional needs. Cry; don't be afraid to shed those tears. There's nothing wrong with tears. And men can shed them too! It doesn't for one minute diminish manhood. I've told that to many men, including my grown sons. Many tears were spilled in the Bible, particularly by the writers of the Psalms. Always, however, the God of all comfort was there with reassurance. At one point David, in great turmoil, cried out, "You have collected all my tears and preserved them in your bottle! You have recorded every one in your book" (Ps. 56:8*b,c* TLB).

David, however, was unwilling to throw in the towel. He may have wept, but he knew God could be depended upon to understand what those tears were all about. David didn't hang up his harp on the willow trees; he didn't unstring it and lay it aside. He kept it and himself in tune by singing and encouraging himself in God; he didn't look to people or circumstances surrounding him. It was God's providence—His power and promises—that David trusted in.

Our tears are not lost to God; they are sealed among His treasures. God will reckon with those who have caused tears to come from His people's eyes. Prayer and tears, David has told us, are good weapons as we face that which shakes us to the very roots of our faith. In many places throughout the Bible, we read of God saying, "I have seen thy tears." He is not a God of caprice, answering then and refusing now. Just remember,

God doesn't hand out medals to those who do not weep. Weeping is a very valid, healthy, and normal emotion. God made us with sensitive natures and the capacity to feel and experience emotions and grief. Even Jesus wept.

The eighth thing I learned was not to fear change. There are times when you have to uproot, move on, dare to be different, to accept the challenge of something new. Sometimes what you view as disastrous turns out to be golden opportunities. View these times as periods of reconstruction—be open to change and allow events to evolve. Recognize that there are some events in your life over which you have no control; God provides wonderful opportunities for you to step out in faith and trust Him still more.

You may even opt for some changes in a career. Step out of the shadows and expose yourself to new ideas and situations; seek to gain new insights into yourself. The apostle Paul says that God has entrusted each of us with the ability to do certain things well (see Rom. 12:6). Rethink what has been counterfeit and unproductive in your past; you may want to go to a local college and take some aptitude tests. As I think back to the days when I was groping to find my way as a single, I now realize that I didn't take advantage of the many opportunities that existed to learn new skills and to develop the creative bent within me. Recently an interior decorator complimented me on my home and said, "Helen, you should have pursued a career in interior design." What are *your* unique abilities? It's never too late to move in a new direction; I'm thinking seriously about interior design courses even now.

Evaluate what went wrong in your life, in your marriage; consider carefully the kind of person you have been and want to become, and go for it. Start thinking and acting creatively. Don't allow the residue of past mistakes to hinder you. Are there some old and neglected interests you can revitalize?

The ninth thing I perceived as being of tremendous importance as I sought to regain my footing, was the need to spend more time with my children. I put out a fleece to the Lord. I'm big on fleeces—some people claim they aren't for today, but I found out the opposite. (If you're not sure what a fleece is, read Judges 6:36-40.) I had bravely moved to a new community to be nearer to my job, but my sixteen-year-old daughter wanted to remain behind in order to finish high school there. I was just too lonely in LaCanada, and my eight-year-old son Kraig and I missed Rhonda. I loved our little house—truly a decorator's dream—and had a lot of fun redecorating it. But Kraig and I talked it over, and realized that we really wanted to be back in Fullerton (these are Southern California communities). So we prayed, "Lord, if You want us to move back, sell our house." This was our fleece. We called the real esate agent who had sold us that darling place eight months before and told her to put up the For Sale sign. Up it went, and within days, down it came. Sold!

We moved back to Fullerton into a condominium. The big sadness accompanying that change was that we had to leave our dog Christy behind. But the Lord even took care of that. We had a yard sale and a distinguished-looking gentleman with two children stopped by. In looking over things, he inquired about our gentle dog, who had made friends with his children. I sorrowfully told him she needed a good home. He promptly told me he'd be delighted to provide that. I want to tell you that God takes pleasure in helping His children—even to finding the right home for a beloved pet.

Back in Fullerton, my daughter was once more a part of our family. Kraig became involved in Little League, and once again he was with old classmates. Those were happy days—I never missed a game. How proud I was of my pitcher boy! The children and I drew closer in those days; it had been the right move. We went through a period of healing, and we came out whole.

Sometimes we want to take pain away from people, but that can be destructive. I am reminded of the illustration Nikos Kazantzakis gives in his book *Report to Greco*. He tells of taking a chrysalis from the trunk of a tree and placing it in his palm. Inside the transparent coating he discerns a living thing. It moves, waiting for the moment when it could emerge into the sunlight. Kazantzakis is in a hurry. He decides to help the process along, so he begins blowing his warm breath over the chrysalis. The moving thing squirms gently and keeps coming more and more to life beneath his warm, persistent breath. Slowly the wings disengage themselves from the body, but in the end it is a futile effort—the wings are maimed, and the creature ceases to move—it is as stiff and lifeless as stone. In his hand, Kazantzakis holds not a butterfly, but a carcass.

The process of change is at once painful and sometimes dreadfully slow, but there does come a time when the struggle is over and we can look back—see where we've been, how we've progressed, and be thankful and happy in our present circumstances. Out of the pain we have emerged kinder, more patient, more tolerant of ourselves and others—yes, more loving. We've been in the school of learning, and we've been good pupils. "For it is God who is at work in you, both to will and to work for His good pleasure" (Phil. 2:13 NASB).

We finally emerged from the divorce—the children and I—like butterflies liberated from a cocoon. Our flight into this new life was not without its adjusments, but we were together in a beautiful bond of loving and caring. No longer were we troubled on every side by the tension that existed in the marriage. We grew together in this new venture.

There is a myth about the outcome of a broken home that I want to challenge. It is said that children suffer irreparable harm. We forget how resilient children can be; they can endure trauma, and they can adapt. I don't minimize for one moment the trauma divorce brings, but there is trauma in a home, too, that is beset by constant conflict between husbands and wives. I have always maintained that children are better off with one stable, happy parent than they are with two unhappy parents. I know this is not a popular concept, but in our case, and in the case of others whom I interviewed and who responded to the questionnaire, I found this to be true.

The tenth thing I learned was that I should concentrate more on things of eternal consequence. I already knew this, but now I sensed it in a more profound way. I had been so busy making a living that I had forgotten I also needed to make a life. Futhermore, there hovered in the back of my mind the thought that unless I was married again I'd be unfulfilled, that I'd be missing out on something, that there was more to life. I mistakenly thought that "more" meant another man. I had been programmed to believe that marriage was the ultimate, and in marriage you realized all your hopes and dreams and lived happily ever after. Fulfillment, in other words, meant marriage.

Today, I no longer believe that. Ideally, perhaps yes, but realistically, no. What then is the answer to those troubled by anxiety, feelings of helplessness and hopelessness—some of it brought on by rejection at the hands of other Christians, judgmental criticism, a misunderstanding of God's grace and mercy, fear of the future? For the divorced man or woman, for anyone actually, it is the recognition that life isn't going to be all beauty and joy. God's comfort and love are not necessarily going to come by way of externals—a new car, a new husband or wife, a new home, a new anything. These things might make life more enjoyable but still not provide internal comfort.

God's comfort can make you strong in weakness. He may not take away your problems and He may not remove your particular cross, but He will give you strength to bear it. He may not remove you from the battle, but He will give peace in the midst of personal war. He does not always remove adversity, but He gives courage to endure. Darkness and light, joy and sorrow, success and suffering—all of these are indispensable strands in the texture of existence. But in and through it all, here is the ultimate answer: "Hope in God" (Ps. 42:5).

It is not people, or one particular person—the man or woman of your dreams—but it is the power and help that come from God. It has been proven that hope moves a person out of depression or suicidal preoccupation.

"Why art thou cast down, O my soul?" the psalmist asked. And we ask it too. "Why art thou disquieted in me? Why downcast? Why be discouraged and sad? Why be depressed and gloomy? Trust in God! Praise him for his wondrous help; he will make you smile again" (paraphrase of Ps. 42:5; 43:5). Yes, I strongly recommend this: *"Hope in God."*

Notes

1. J. Wallace Hamilton, *What About Tomorrow?* (Old Tappan, N.J.: Fleming H. Revell Co., 1972).

2. Gladys Lindberg and Judy McFarland, *Take Charge of Your Health* (San Francisco: Harper & Row, 1981). I had the privilege of living with Mrs. Lindberg for three months while assisting in the development of this book. My endorsement of her approach to nutrition and taking care of your health is based on firsthand knowledge. I have followed her health principles for most of my adult life.

Chapter Nine

LONELINESS
Becoming Wounded Healers

Henry Nouwen in *The Wounded Healer* describes "the wound of loneliness" as being like "the Grand Canyon"—a deep incision in the surface of our existence that has become an inexhaustible source of beauty and self-understanding. Nouwen says, "Therefore I would like to voice loudly and clearly what might seem unpopular and maybe even disturbing. The Christian way of life does not take away our loneliness; it protects and cherishes it as a precious gift."[1]

I can almost hear you protest. "Loneliness, a precious gift! You don't know what you are talking about if you agree with Nouwen." In or out of marriage we can feel lonely. Nouwen says, for instance, that many celibates live with the naïve dream that in the intimacy of marriage their loneliness will be taken away. Ideally, yes, but realistically, no. In this regard, I am very much in agreement with Jay Adams and his fine discourse on "What Marriage Is All About" (see his book, chapter 2). Marriage was established because Adam was alone, and God said that wasn't good (Gen. 2:18). As stated in an earlier chapter, companionship, therefore, is the essence of marriage. Adams explains that sin has so distorted society and so twisted human beings in their relationships to God and to one another that some do live lonely lives despite God's rule (regarding marriage in Gen. 2:24—leaving one's father and mother to cleave to one's wife, or husband, and becoming one) and the rule's provision (see *Marriage, Divorce, and Remarriage* by

Adams, p. 8). Those of us who have been married and divorced would be quick to tell the unmarried that marriage is not a cure-all for the loneliness syndrome. Ask those who have lived through a failed marital relationship why the marriage ended up as another divorce statistic. There is a strong likelihood that they will tell you the marriage was ruined because their partner failed to take their loneliness away. But the possibility exists that we can come to regard loneliness as a precious gift, whether we are married or single.

Questionnaire responses showed a recurring theme—the deep sadness that Christians experienced on the other side of divorce, the feeling that somehow they had let God down. The Bible tells us that through Christ who strengthens us we can do all things (Phil. 4:13). Then why weren't we able to continue in the marriage relationship, and why, once divorced, did we find it so difficult to deal with the loneliness? These were questions the respondents asked themselves.

LONELINESS AND ALONENESS

Writer Gary P. Putnam made some perceptive comments on loneliness. "All of us are lonely at some times in our life. But loneliness need not be a way of life for us. The separation loneliness brings can be overcome by bridges of understanding between ourselves and others."[2] I know of many singles who are doing this. Bridge-building takes time and effort; in the process our thoughts are removed from our own lonely state as we reach out to touch someone else who is lonely too.

I have often said that loneliness is the price we pay for noninvolvement. Loneliness is actually the word we use to express the pain of being alone. Putnam defines loneliness as to be without significant others and to wish it were otherwise. He relates an incident that helped him understand aloneness and loneliness. It happened when he called on a woman in the hospital—a woman who suffered an illness that brought her to the brink of death. "There I was about to die," she told Putnam, "nothing I had previously valued really mattered. . . . And God was all that there was."[3]

But He is a God who is enough.

Putnam's observations about that incident are very perceptive. "For all our clamoring about community—how people
need one another, there are still those frequent moments when
we are alone before life's biggest questions. Guilt, inferiority,
temptation, grief, and ultimately death are all issues we
confront alone and lonely."[4]

Which is another way of saying that we must come to terms
with ourselves if we are to deal with loneliness. I have told my
children on many occasions that I have to live with myself, and
so, I want to be fit for myself to know. That's a full-time job!

Paul Tournier, M.D., in his book, *Escape from Loneliness,* says
that every doctor knows what the terrible loneliness of modern
man is. Often people's physical problems are only symptoms, of
deeper, more serious problems—their emotional and mental
distress. And much of this is caused by living in isolation.

Dr. Tournier tells of a woman who was secretary of an
international organization. Her work was appreciated, and she
received every courtesy. Many visitors from every country
came to her office, but they spoke only about business. Never
was there a word addressed to her as a person. She lived in a
great modern building, with countless one-room flats, where
the neighbors' noises came from every floor. She knew none of
these neighbors, even though she rubbed shoulders with them
in the elevator daily. And she had no intimate friends. Her
office was even in the same building where she lived, so she
didn't have to leave it to go home, and she rarely went out for
any reason except for a hurried shopping trip. Before falling
asleep at night, she would switch on the radio just to hear the
closing words from a certain speaker on a regular program:
"And so, we bid you a very pleasant good night!" *It was a
human voice, speaking to her.*[5]

EMOTIONAL ISOLATION

Such isolation comes about because of many things. Some
people become victims of isolation because they have become
alienated from family members—this happens often in divorce
cases. Many families, even today when divorce has become

commonplace, simply cannot handle divorce. Individuals, alienated even from loved ones, lead lonely, discouraging lives, with only, perhaps, a dog or cat for company. I know this is happening in the complex where I now live. I see these people every day as I sit here typing. One woman in particular comes to mind. I smile when she walks by, but it is actually very sad. It would be funny and make a darling cartoon if it weren't so pathetic. She pushes her dog in a baby stroller!

"Emotional isolation of modern men," Tournier says, is brought about in part, because we are no longer as controlled by social class as we once were. By this is meant the family in transition, our rootlessness, the anonymity of the large city and big business, and the contradictory ideologies so prevalent today. Many people have cut themselves loose from their early religious moorings and have lost "the community of faith and of moral, spiritual, and social ideas brought about by the church—all of which gave a framework to individual life."[6] Tournier also refers to what was once so highly regarded—"the indissolubility of the marital bonds plus the filial respect imposed by tradition."[7] In our own country, the family has always been the mainstay of our society, but this appears to be changing. And not only are the demographics changing, but our attitudes have changed radically.

One of the things that disburbed Tournier the most was "parents in conflict" and how this tends, in children, to foster isolation and mistrust. He speaks of the "terrifying memories of parental fights," which are the most recurring factor found in the histories of "the anxious and withdrawn who come to consult us."[8] He says:

It takes love, tact, and much time in order to help them break down walls behind which they have imprisoned themselves. . . . The children are at stake in any parental conflict. they are, in turn, spoiled and threatened, praised and disparaged, exposed to all the contradictions and about turns brought on by the ups and downs of the tragic conflict. One moment understanding, a moment later they see all too clearly what their parents are about. . . .

Many children have given me the memoirs of their childhood to read, written in order to unburden their heart. They do not dare publish them for fear of shaming the family. If only parents in conflict could read such poignant pages, their eyes might be opened to the unknown sufferings they are sowing for all of life in the soul of their child."[9]

How significant this all is—how much we need to recognize as individuals (and as the church) that we bring into our marriages remnants of things that have happened to us in the past—often from our childhood experiences, things we had no control over, things we are not even aware of that have shaped our reactions to our own marriages. Many marriages are deeply hurt by personal idiosyncrasies in individual partners—things that may not have shown up in courtship days. Some of these problems and habits carried over into a marriage can destroy love and the marriage itself.

Tournier points to many couples, however, who never opt for divorce and who sincerely believe that they have kept their marital conflict unknown to their children. "But children are never fooled by the lie. They see through the parents' unconscious, yes, even sincere lies."[10] This then has repercussions upon the children's own relationships. Some of them have never experienced good role models in family relationships—especially that between their mother and father—and they themselves live in isolation in their own marriages. Of this, Tournier states, "The bizarre behavior, distant and yet pitiable, to which the wounds of their childhood experience push them only further contributes to isolate them in life."[11]

THE LONGING TO BE MARRIED

But this feeling of loneliness doesn't strike only at the nervous and the withdrawn; it is widespread and, according to Tournier, "is the result of the spirit of our age."[12] How much we in the church need to be aware of this—how much we need to hear this and be sensitive to what is happening to so many who walk into our churches on Sunday. From 1950 to 1983, the number of people who lived alone—whether out of choice or necessity—went from four million to more than nineteen million, an increase of nearly 400 percent.[13] That's a lot of people who are alone. God said that wasn't good—remember?—and for the church to say that such as these who are divorced "should purpose not to remarry" strikes me as being terribly insensitive to their plight and to what God Himself said. Many of the people I've talked to and who responded to the questionnaire stated that they sincerely had tried remaining single, but after being married for so many years, accustomed to having someone else around, the transition was more than they could handle. The men who didn't retain custody of their children particularly felt the loneliness.

Dr. Tournier believes that the greater divorce occurring these days is "between the elite and the people."[14] He explains this in reference to the church. "This tragic isolation of the elite is present most acutely in the church, especially in the Protestant Church. Among religious people there are many of a deep spirituality who could and should help the world to awaken to its soul and to put an end to its tremendous moral confusion. However, they move in a world of their own, speak a language of their own, and in their passion for sincerity, part company with each other along a thousand different ways."[15] He explains that he has rarely felt the modern man's isolation more grippingly than in his encounters with deaconesses or church pastors who are carried away with the activism rampant in their churches, holding meeting upon meeting, and so burdened with programs that they have little if any time for pastoral care.[16]

Yet, "it is the church, alone, nevertheless, which can answer the world of today's tremendous thirst for community,"[17] Tournier points out, urging believers to get back to the biblical pattern outlined in Acts 4:32; 2:44.

One woman confided that she was so anxious for happiness and remarriage that she had resorted to looking at the obituary columns in the newspaper. When she'd find the name of a woman who had died, she'd try to figure out how old that woman must have been and if she had a remaining husband, who he was and what he did. Then she'd start dreaming: maybe she could run into him at a local restaurant some evening. Surely he'd be going out to eat a lot of his meals now that he was a widower. She hated to admit it, but she was desperate for companionship having become so accustomed to marriage (she'd been married for more than twenty years). Finally she realized that marriage wasn't necessarily the answer, but that coming to terms with herself first was necessary for inner healing. And God could bring that about. Happiness wasn't the goal, but the blessedness of a right relationship with Him was. But wouldn't it have been wonderful for her if she could have felt comfortable going to her church instead of to the newspaper obituary column?

It's ironic that many married people envy those who are unmarried. They fantasize about what it must be like to be footloose and fancy-free and dating once again. The strange thing about such dreams is that they don't include thoughts of what it's like for that man or woman in his or her state of aloneness.

When I was once again single, I fantasized about being married again, but it was only about being happily married. The single life looms as desirable to those who are unhappily married, and thoughts of marriage occupy a part of our thinking when we are single. We seem to forget that there is a price to pay whether single or married. The reason, of course, is that we are always stuck with ourselves. Until we have come to terms with ourselves, we make pretty miserable company.

What are some of the things we miss about marriage? Probably adult dialogue and someone to share the day's events and problems with would be at the top of many people's list. It could also be called intellectual companionship. One woman mentioned she missed having someone to sleep with every night; someone else said he missed spending weekends together. Another person related he didn't like eating alone. What it amounts to really is sharing life with someone on a daily basis.

A number of people mentioned that a good demanding job is a great solace for loneliness. I think what these individuals are saying is that busyness helps to cover up the pain of being alone, but even so, with a divorce you come home to four walls, as one lonely, divorced man expressed it. He went on to talk about the silences he experienced when there was no one around to talk to, even though he and his wife hadn't communicated too well. "Yes, the silences—that's difficult," he said.

FULFILLMENT: WHAT IS IT?

Marriage is not necessarily the answer to complete fulfillment. It is really too much to ask or expect of any one other person that they fulfill us ultimately. Ultimate satisfaction, in the final analysis, comes from living at peace with yourself and God. Until you have made that peace, you are not ready for remarriage. Only after I had been alone for three years and felt I was making a good adjustment to life as a solo, was I ready for remarriage. I have often said that if I had not met my husband, and the circumstances came together as they did, I believe I could have remained single. In talking to several divorced women, I have learned that they now feel that way about themselves. One woman has been divorced four years, another nine years, still another eleven years. It seems that the longer you live alone, the more you realize there are distinct advantages in singleness. The wise individual will grasp them and make them work for his or her best interests. It is not being selfish to seek what is best for yourself and for your children at this stage in your life. Actually, it's called survival.

If you don't think of yourself and take care of yourself now, who will? You owe it to yourself and to your children to pick up the strands of your life and make something out of them. One of the fringe benefits of being handed back your life is being awarded custody of yourself. Often we mistakenly think we will find fulfillment, inner peace, and satisfaction *with* someone, but the kind of deep, settled inner peace that is the ultimate in satisfaction is something that no mere human being can ever do for us—regardless how wonderful he or she might be.

The day came for me, as it does for most divorced individuals, when I understood that there were worse things than being alone and unmarried. I finally confronted my inner memories and the pain. I faced my own contribution to the failure of the marriage and asked for God's forgiveness, and I acknowledged my part in the failure of the relationship to my former husband. I had to forgive myself too. In doing these things, I was taking steps to make it possible for God to bring about "beauty for ashes." Those wounds needed cleansing and healing; then I could get on with living. Until we have done this cleansing and healing, we are not ready for remarriage.

It is a mistake to think of being single and alone as a state of deprivation. We can be as much at the mercy of others outside of marriage, as within it, however, and we are much more vulnerable when we are alone, so we are well advised to watch it. But being single affords opportunities to rediscover who we really are. This fear of being alone panics some. But several people spoke of this time as a time of rejuvenation in discovering themselves.

THE BENEFITS OF THE SINGLE LIFE

To be alone is to place ourselves in the position of being able to draw closer to God. We can do that. If we choose to do that, I can assure you He will prove Himself to be the God who is enough. There are some who draw back, afraid that God will reveal things to them about themselves that they'd rather not confront. How much they are depriving themselves of help and hope.

Jay Adams points out that God has called some men and women to be exceptions to His own rule (regarding marriage and that it is "not good" to be alone) and has provided for their need of companionship by gifting them especially to lead the single life (cf. Matt. 19:11, 12; I Cor. 7:7). According to these verses, God has singled out for Himself some people to lead lives of celibacy for the sake of His Kingdom. Jesus talked about this with His disciples. You may recall the incident. After the discussion about divorce (Matt. 19:3-9), in which Jesus pointed out that fornication (sexual sin) was the only permissible ground for divorce among believers, the disciples, quick to pick up on the implications of this, and not yet understanding the implications of His pardoning grace (that would cover even marital failure), responded, "If that is how it is, it is better not to marry" (v. 10 TLB).

Adams puts it like this: "They thought, presumably, if marriage is that permanent, it would be better not to run the risk of marrying the wrong person" (see p. 9, *Marriage, Divorce, and Remarriage*).

In reply Jesus said, "Not everyone can accept this statement" (v. 11 TLB), and He goes on to urge those to whom this ability has been given, to accept this as a gift—the gift of celibacy from God. The apostle Paul talks about this also in I Corinthians 7:7. Paul amplifies this somewhat by implying that one of the better ways to live a satisfying (not lonely) life is to become involved in the work of the Lord in ways that married persons oftentimes cannot (cf. I Cor. 7:33-34). "The single life is not according to the rule set forth in Genesis 2:18; it is exceptional," Jay Adams emphasizes, and I think he is correct in his amplification of this. (I would urge readers who need more help with this to seek out his book and study chapter 2 in particular.)

What I see in all of this, however, is that for most of us, especially once we've been married, it is difficult to remain single forever. However, being alone can mean more interesting lives as we expand our interests in different directions. I know that being alone can be like a life without mirrors, that the hours can seem dehydrated at times, and that at other times the pain of living alone is like living in a graveyard of broken dreams. Many of the questionnaire respondents spoke of feeling like they were living alone even when they were married. They were dependent on the services each provided the other without ever really sharing their lives and hearts. So there is much to be said for being in the single state after a divorce rather than in an unhappy married state.

Some, after making the leap into the single life, and making a good adjustment, find they don't want to risk being hurt again, and so they opt for the single state. Many find that when they finally accept that their marriages have come to an end, but that it's not the end of their lives, then they are able to restructure their lives. It can be a rich life intellectually and socially when you are alone, but sometimes, admittedly, it's emotionally hit or miss. Someone described it as feeling like you are playing musical chairs, but every time they stop the music, you're the one who's out. And that it's hard to be brave twenty-four hours a day on your own.

Some people go through life being a part of the problem; others are part of the solution. Some people choose roads that lead forward; others choose roads that lead backward. I remember interviewing Wallace Johnson, multimillionaire builder and co-founder of Holiday Inns International, shortly after my divorce, and asking him how he had achieved so much. Among other things, he laughingly said, "Helen, if you are ever going to fall, make certain you fall forward; it never has seemed to me to make much sense to fall backward." I took that bit of advice to heart. It makes sense, that not much can be gained by a lot of morbid retrospection and a lot of "if only" thinking.

In my speaking during that time, I urged women to let Christ's love forgive their past, to let His peace take over their present, and to let His will be their will for today and the unknown future. I caught on one day that I'd better practice what I was preaching!

Putting that attitude into practice does wonders in alleviating loneliness. It is the realization that you've placed yourself in God's hands, and He can be trusted to work out for you what is best for the present and the future. It is the better par)t of wisdom to discard the spirit of despair and mourning, and to don the garment of praise. Life is for living; let us dare to live. God may not prevent us from becoming lonely at times in our lives, but the great good news is that He has told us, "I am with you."

In business circles we hear much talk of "hands-on management," the idea that once a situation is analyzed, appropriate steps need to be taken to bring about desired and needed change. This is, in effect, what we do when we decide we need to get on with living, and when we finally opt for a divorce. I am reminded of one of Arthur Miller's plays, *The Misfits*, where Roslyn meets her husband on the steps of the courthouse. He asks her, "Why do we have to be divorced?" Her answer reveals the experience of many when she says, "If I am going to be alone, I want to be alone by myself."

ALONE AGAIN

Richards Krebs, writing in *Alone Again,* reminds us that Jesus wants us to bang on His Father's door. If, for instance, you are having trouble letting go of a lost mate, tell God about it. If you are lonely and frightened, holler at Him for help. If you are bewildered by the problems you have to cope with, call out to the Father, ask Him to help you choose wisely.

Krebs says, "When you are in trouble on your journey, take Jesus seriously. You will find that He meant what He said about His Father. More importantly, you will find that He also meant these words: 'I am with you always. . . . ' He meant these words for you."[18]

Dr. Paul Tournier believes that "alone, a person gets more hopelessly entangled," that we, in fact, need the spirit of fellowship.[19] "There are certain blessings found only in fellowship and in total surrender to one's church."[20] Christianity offers the resources of God's grace, of daily fellowship with Christ, and all that we need for inner renewal in order to face the obstacles and traps that lie in our path. But we also desperately need the fellowship of people. We need the companionship and fellowship of "wounded healers." How well I recall at one time praying, in my lonely aloneness, "Oh God, I need someone with a face on!"

USING OUR LONELINESS TO HELP OTHERS

In his book, *The Wounded Healer,* Nouwen observes that the Christian leader is a man (or woman) of God only insofar as he or she is able to make the compassion of God credible in his or her own world. The compassionate man or woman points to the possibility of forgiveness, thus helping others to free themselves from the chains of their restrictive shame, restoring their hope for the future as they look into the face of Him in whose image we are all shaped.

Nouwen makes the disturbing observation that if there is any posture that disturbs a suffering man or woman, it is aloofness. The tragedy of Christian ministry is that many who are in great need, many who seek an attentive ear, a word of support, a forgiving embrace, a firm hand, a tender smile, or even a stuttering confession of inability to do more often find their ministers distant people who do not want to get burned with other people's problems. They are unable or, more likely, unwilling to express their feelings of affection, anger, and hostility.

When I was struggling with loneliness, I accumulated quite a library of books on the subject. You can search them out, too, and they will provide some helpful insights. Books are always good companions; I never felt alone when I was reading a good book. It's one of the better ways to fill up lonely hours. A good book and good music—two beautiful companions.

In more recent years, I met Luci Swindoll and read her book *Wide My World, Narrow My Bed* with the subtitle *Living and Loving the Single Life.*[21] Luci is single by choice, and her perspective is that the single life is great. It's fulfilling. And it can be the basis for a very special relationship with God. Among the may things that Luci suggests as making for a richer single life are cultivating a love of good books and good music, developing an interest in the arts, being hospitable, developing a sense of humor, and making good friends. Luci, to my way of thinking, is a "wounded healer." She admits to knowing what it's like to be lonely and that we can become victims of a destructive thought process whereby we wallow in self-pity because there is nobody there to share the load.

Another person whose name I see a lot in Christian magazines and who is closely identified with the Christian single's movement is Harold Ivan Smith. I became acquainted with Harold when his book, *Tear-Catchers*, was still in the thinking stages.[22] I remember how we talked in my office and how we encouraged each other. The subtitle of his book is "Developing the Gift of Compassion," and the book is a rich expression of his own experience with tears, encouraging readers to overcome their reluctance to weep, and recognizing that we are supposed to cry. Smith urges us to understand and accept the natural release of tears as a way to emotional and spiritual health, and then to use this compassionate gift as a bridge so that wounded people can be healed.

"BEAUTY FOR ASHES"

The prophet Isaiah declared that the Spirit of the Lord came upon him and the Lord had anointed him to bring good news to the suffering and afflicted. He was to comfort the brokenhearted, to announce liberty to captives, and to open the eyes of the blind. He was to tell those in mourning that the time of God's favor had come and that God would give:

> Beauty for ashes;
> Joy instead of mourning;
> Praise instead of heaviness (Isa. 61:1-3 TLB).

Other versions speak of "binding up the brokenhearted." Brokenhearted people are usually lonely people. Unquestionably, loneliness is one of the most painful of human wounds.

As I look at divorced-remarried Christians, I see repeatedly that those who have been judged as failures and shunned by many in the Christian community are the very ones who understand best what being a wounded healer is all about. They are allowing their own wounds to be the source of healing for others. Out of their struggles with loneliness and despair, they have come to understand themselves better. Like the old-time prophet, they can offer others that which they have learned— drawing from the wellspring of their own experience.

At a luncheon where I spoke shortly after my divorce was final, I shared the painful experience I was going through, struggling with loneliness, and seeking to find my identity again as a single woman with children. It was a difficult assignment—my wounds were still very fresh. Yet, I had been told that many others in that room were going through the same or some kind of pain. Afterwards, a weeping woman handed me a slip of paper. On it were these words: "Our sympathy is never very deep unless founded on our feelings. We pity, but do not enter into the grief which we have never felt." How much those words meant to me! I pondered them for days as I came to understand that I, too, could be "a wounded healer."

I closely identified with the psalmist who knew what it was to quake inwardly, but who poured out his thoughts and innermost feelings. The book of Psalms reveals David as "a wounded healer."

WHAT BEING "A WOUNDED HEALER"
IS ALL ABOUT

In Jerusalem, the night before Christ's crucifixion, alone with His beloved disciples, Jesus prayed for these men, and gave them a promise. He had already warned them of the enmity they could expect from the world, and then He added an important "but." Jesus said, "But I still send you the Comforter—the Holy Spirit, the source of all truth" (John 15:26*a* TLB). This promise was not meant for just those disciples; it is for us also. Here is the resource we need in our times of loneliness and despair. Here is Jesus Himself, in the presence of the blessed Holy Spirit, acting on our behalf as *the* "wounded healer." He does not want us to walk through life alone and lonely.

At another time in Jesus' life, He dined at Matthew's house. The Pharisees were indignant. They knew there were some notorious swindlers there as guests. They asked the disciples, "Why does your teacher associate with men like that?" (Matt. 9:11 TLB).

Jesus took it upon Himself to answer their question—it wasn't the answer they expected. "Because people who are well don't need a doctor! It's the sick people who do!" . . . Then He added, "Now go away and learn the meaning of this verse of Scripture, 'It isn't your sacrifices and your gifts I want—I want you to be merciful' " (vv. 12, 13).

Jesus exhibited in His own words and actions the prophetic word of Hosea; "I desire mercy, and not sacrifice" (Hos. 9:6 AV). What Jesus came to do, He empowers His disciples to continue to do—and that includes us. The way of mercy requires that we be His "wounded healers" to the divorced among us and to those who want to remarry.

I am reminded of the story of a little girl who arrived home late from playing with a friend. Upon questioning, the mother learned that the little playmate was feeling sad because her doll was broken. "So I helped her," the tardy little girl explained to her mother.

"How did you help her?" asked the mother.

"Well, I just sat down and cried with her."

How thankful I was in my lonely, sad moments when two very special friends sat and comforted me, or when I could call them and receive their help, counsel, and encouragement. While it is true that we can expect to lose many friends when we go through the divorce experience (some of them will drop by the wayside, if we remarry, too), still I was the recipient of the love and understanding of a number of individuals especially as I began to make the effort myself to reach out to others. I discovered for myself the meaning in the Apostle Paul's exhortation that we practice hospitality. That's what being a tear-catcher, a wounded healer is about. To hole up in your own four-square world is not the way out of loneliness. "Alone we find solitude, Together we find love," says a sensitive poet.[23]

Dr. Tournier explains that doctors daily discover the loneliness of men and women, and what they are seeing is that "loneliness is linked with fear. Men fear one another, fear to be crushed in life, fear to be misunderstood. The doctor knows that fear is a universal and natural feeling, though everyone seeks to hide it. . . .

"Thus, fear breeds loneliness and conflict; loneliness and conflict breed fear. To heal the world, we must give men an answer to fear and restore among them the sense of community."[24]

As wounded healers, we respond to the needs of others by seeking ways to help and restore them. The apostle Paul said, "Dear brothers, if a Christian is overcome by some sin, you who are godly should gently and humbly help him back onto the right path, remembering that next time it might be one of you who is in the wrong. Share each other's troubles and problems, and so obey our Lord's command. If anyone thinks he is too great to stoop to this, he is fooling himself. He is really a nobody. . . . Each of us must bear some faults and burdens of his own. For none of us is perfect!" (Gal. 6:1-3, 5 TLB).

Loneliness, says Henri Nouwen, is a sort of "sweet pain."

How can that be? I think of my precious friend, Rosie, who embraces her loneliness and, at the same time, reaches out to embrace lonely others. Because we confront our pain, and come to understand it, we can better hold out the promise of healing to others as we relate to them that the touch of the Great Physician brings healing to wounds. In this way our pain becomes the "precious gift" described at the outset of this chapter. Rosie's husband deserted her and her daughter, running off to sail around the world with another woman. But Rosie is a Christian. Her husband was not. Rosie has put her own faith and doubt, her own hope and despair, her own light and darkness, her own loneliness and wounds, at the disposal of those who need to find a way through the confusion and complexities—the pain and uncertainty in their lives.

That's what being a wounded healer is all about. Many singles I know have used their pain to help others—to build bridges between lonely people. In the process their thoughts are removed from their own lonely state.

Why have I devoted so many pages to a discussion of this subject? Because the divorced-remarried persons to whom I have talked and who responded to the questionnaire pointed to loneliness as having been their number one wound. Their inner loneliness revealed to them an inner emptiness that could have been destructive if misunderstood. As divorced lonely people, alienated from so many who did not understand their situation, it would have been so easy at times to just give up, and at other times to give in to the temptations of the world. Yet those of us who walked on, who chose Jesus as our companion in our loneliness, discovered that "no love or friendship, no intimate embrace or tender kiss, no community, no other man or woman," would be able to satisfy our desire to be released from our lonely condition. We might have hoped that one day the right man or woman would come into our lives—someone who would understand our expectations—or that a better job would fulfill us and take away our loneliness. These false hopes lead us to make exhausting demands of others, as well as ourselves, and only produce bitterness, frustration, dashed hopes, and dangerous hostility, when the truth is that nobody, and nothing, can live up to *all* our expectations. The way out of loneliness is to accept it and then to reach out to others who are just as hurt and lonely.

Paul Tournier says, "The elite of the gospel is not made up of the 'advanced,' but of poor devils who accept God's grace."[25] There are a lot of us "poor devils" in the Christian community.

Notes

1. Henri J. M. Nouwen, *The Wounded Healer* (Garden City, N.Y.: Doubleday, Image Books, 1979), p. 84.
2. Gary P. Putnam, "Loneliness: And God Was All That There Was," *Divorce,* published by the North American Conference of Separated and Divorced Catholics, Summer 1978, p. 9.
3. Ibid.
4. Ibid.
5. Paul Tournier, *Escape from Loneliness* (Philadelphia: Westminster Press, 1972), p. 13.
6. Ibid., p. 20.
7. Ibid.
8. Ibid., p. 18.
9. Ibid., pp. 18, 19.
10. Ibid., p. 19.
11. Ibid.
12. Ibid., p. 20.
13. According to Peter Stein, a sociologist and author of *Single Life.*
14. Tournier, p. 22.
15. Ibid.
16. Ibid., p. 23.
17. Ibid.
18. Richard Krebs, *Alone Again* (Minneapolis: Augsburg Publishing House, 1978), p. 124.
19. Tournier, p. 56.
20. Ibid., p. 26.
21. Luci Swindoll, *Wide My World, Narrow My Bed* (Portland, Ore.: Multnomah Press, 1982).
22. Harold Ivan Smith, *Tear-Catchers* (Nashville: Abingdon Press, 1984).
23. Walter Rinder, *Love Is an Attitude* (Millbrae, Calif.: Celestial Arts Publishing, 1970).
24. Tournier, pp. 26, 27.
25. Ibid., p. 84.

Chapter Ten

Peace Without Compromise

A young woman once asked Saint Francis whether or not it was a sin to use rouge. He cocked his head and said, "Well, some theologians claim it's all right; others disagree."

Not satisfied, the young lady pushed him still further. "That's all very well, but what should *I* do—use rouge or not?"

"Why not follow the middle course?" Saint Francis replied. "Rouge only one cheek."

I suppose that young woman thought she had problems—and undoubtedly for her day, that was a problem. But her "solution" was compromise—when you try to keep everyone happy, but are not experiencing happiness yourself. Compromise tries to keep peace with others, but does not let you live with peace yourself.

From the growing number of divorces among the Christian community, it can be seen that many people have come to the conclusion that they are unwilling to live a life of compromise. I am reminded of a well-known Christian woman whose divorce became final a few years ago. The fact that she was so well-known caused a ripple of comment. Perhaps it would be more accurate to say it was a tidal wave of comment. But when and if she ever considers remarriage, the present tidal wave of criticism will seem mild in comparison.

Her secretary, in describing my friend's reaction to the finality of the divorce, stated, "She's happy. I know it sounds terrible, but she hasn't been exactly happy for a long, long time. In contrast to what she's been, I would have to say she's happy now."

Perhaps peaceful would have been a more accurate word. When you have lived in unpeace for a long time, the initial reaction after the divorce is one of peace. That is not easy to explain to those looking in from the outside. The feeling is the result of a combination of things—you have removed yourself from the scene of battle, for one thing. So, of course, there is peace. The conflict has been left behind.

One critical writer on the subject of divorce has said that retreat is never the road to victory. This same writer believes that separation is the better way to go, for that places you in an arena where you can develop a new understanding of yourself and your spouse. Recently, following my appearance on the Toronto TV program "100 Huntley Street," a woman caller specifically asked to speak to me. She related that she and her husband had been separated eleven years and the prospects for getting together were no better now than they had been at the time they separated.

"How peaceful is it living like that?" I asked her.

"Are you kidding!" she said in a horrified tone of voice. "There is no peace."

Frankly, I do not regard such separation as an answer to marital conflict. Is that what God expects and wants for His children? It seems to me that if after a period of evaluating one's situation and prayerfully seeking to bring about change, one's marriage or separation situation still remains so sub-ideal, seeking a divorce cannot be called "retreating."

The feeling of peace that my divorced friend experienced can also be explained as a feeling of relief that now the uncertainty about whether to go ahead with the divorce or not is over, and a realization that the possibility for a different future is in sight. But those "happy," or peaceful feelings will give away every so often to guilt and anxiety as my friend progresses along the path of those who are formerly marrieds.

PEACE AND OUR CHILDREN

As she looks back (which she cannot help but do from time to time) and views the wreckage of the marriage and the havoc this creates at times for herself and for her children, she will have mixed feelings.

One of the worst ways we have of handling our guilt relates to our children. We try to compensate to them for what we subconsciously feel we have done by depriving them of their father (or mother). It's as if we are buying their favor by our favors. A father, for instance, who has weekend visiting privileges with his children may lavish gifts and good times upon them. Children are quick to recognize a good thing and will take advantage of such indulgences. What is the father actually doing? He's trying to assuage his own guilt over the failure of the marriage.

The mother, who is quite often given custody of the children, can easily do the same thing. She may extend TV privileges beyond what, in her heart, she knows is good for the child, or she will let the children's coaxing wear down her resistance and give in to their demands.

Children can become adept at pitting one parent against the other. The immediate effects may not be too noticeable, but the long-range effects can be devastating for all concerned. Particularly when remarriage occurs, the guilt level can rise alarmingly fast. At this juncture, obviously, more than the child and parent are involved—now there is the stepfather (or stepmother), and the problems become compounded very fast.

Visible or tangible signs of a parent's affection are not always accurate barometers of a parent's real love at all. They are more like bribes in these tangled emotional situations!

We may fail to remember just how flexible children really are and that they can bend quite easily with life's inequities. Our overreacting can result in spoiled children who go through life expecting everything to be handed to them on a silver platter. Unless we have learned how to handle our hurts and our guilt *before* remarriage, these crisscrossed relationships can pose a whole new set of problems that we did not encounter in our first marriages.

In order to live with our conscience, it stands to reason that we will not do those things that violate a good conscience. With regard to our children, this means a conscious effort to make certain we do not demean the child's father (or mother) in his or her presence. The formerly married have an insidious way of getting back at their ex-spouses through their children. There are dozens of ways this is done: by spoiling vacations and visit plans; by failing to give the child a message from the other parent (if such a message comes in the child's absence); saying disparaging things about the ex and the ex's family (the child's grandparents, aunts, uncles, cousins); rehashing what contributed to the marital failure in the presence of the child, etc.

If we would free ourselves of guilt over the effects of our divorces and remarriages on our children, then we must avoid pulling strings and making marionettes out of these children. We shouldn't use the children as carrier pigeons insisting that they relate what is going on in the other parent's new marriage. Instead, concentrate on helping the children to think well of their fathers (mothers) and his (her) family, and seek ways to make certain there is a good ongoing relationship with them.

From my own experience I can relate to you that this is possible. In fact, on visits to Southern California (where my former husband and his family live), I make certain that I at least call them if I cannot go to see them. At first it was somewhat awkward, but with the passing of the years that has disappeared. Moreover, I communicate with them by telephone. I had worked at maintaining an open relationship with them through the early years following the divorce because I knew it would ease the situation for all concerned, but specially for the children. But the credit for this does not belong to myself only—to their credit, my former husband and his family accepted my overtures and recognized that it was for the greater good of all concerned. Not only have the children benefited, but all our lives have been enriched by this ongoing relationship.

For many years, when we lived out of state, my husband and I saw to it that my growing son was flown back to California at Christmastime and for spring vacation. During the summers, I flew him up to Canada to be with his married sister. There were times, because of this expenditure, that my husband and I had to go without a vacation ourselves. I relate this to illustrate that to live with a good conscience free from guilt requires some effort, and may even require some sacrificing. Is family life an institution that is to endure? Frankly, I believe it is irreplaceable. But in these difficult areas of "blended families" with stepfather and stepmother relationships, we owe it to our children to help them adjust to the inevitable tensions that result when divorce and remarriage enter the picture, taking them through these crisis times with as much ease as possible. To allow them to interact and continue their parent-child relationships with the missing parent without trauma is terribly important. It is the height of selfishness to deprive them of this, adding more anxiety and stress to their lives.

PEACE AND OUR IN-LAWS

If you would live at peace with yourself, you will recognize that your children didn't ask to be born. Whatever it takes, if it is within your power to make it happen, then no effort should be spared to encourage peaceful relationships, even when there has been a disruption in the marriage relationship. Just recently my son's father was hospitalized in a serious condition. I immediately phoned my former in-laws assuring them of our concern and letting them know that I'd put Kraig on a plane immediately, if it was necessary. For several days we communicated this way by phone. While Kraig's father was on his sickbed in the hospital, both my son and I talked to him by phone. We prayed for his father's recovery and rejoiced when he recovered. God is faithful, and God honors when we respond with love and kindness. Ephesians 4:32 is always operative in the life of that one who is seeking to truly live a peaceful Christ-honoring life. To know that you have not been guilty of saying unkind things or seeking revenge in various ways is to be able to live free from guilt and the remorse that this brings.

I know of one woman who flew to another state to visit her ex's favorite aunt. There she unloaded all her stored-up venom, convincing the elderly lady that her nephew had wronged her terribly. The aunt, now up in years and not as capable as she once had been of sorting things out, believed this vicious woman, wrote her nephew telling him she never wanted to hear from him again, that she was ashamed of him. She berated him for stepping out of God's will, for going against the teachings of the Bible, and for deserting his wife. The tragedy of this story is that because the man had never received much love from his mother, this aunt had been as a surrogate mother to him, and when he received the letter from her he was heartbroken. He wrote several letters in reply; he called her on the phone, but she hung up the phone. Finally she wrote him back stating she never wanted to hear from him again. The relationship was severed, never to be restored.

This same woman succeeded in alienating one married son from his father, making it extremely difficult for another married son to maintain a relationship. The point is that she is representative of those whose children and other family members fall victim to the tragedy of divorce because of her own unwillingness to confront the reality of her part in the marriage failure.

But what of those situations where the problems in the first marriage were so difficult as to make it next to impossible to handle one's relationship to the former mate and his or her family in a gracious way? And what about those situations where child-support money or alimony isn't forthcoming?

After you have done all within your human power to right the wrongs and to seek ways to communicate harmoniously, and as you have sought God's help in how to go about this, you have no recourse but to leave it all in God's hands. I believe God wants us, however, to do our part. I always say to do the thing near at hand, the right thing, and then leave the results with God. I do not have much patience, I must confess, with that divorced parent who fails to comply in sending child support payments, or alimony to a woman struggling to make ends meet. It is precisely at this point where the church has one of its finest opportunities to show true godly compassion—sadly, not all churches are so responding.

I know a woman who left her husband because he was

abusive to their children. Nothing could be quite as bad as she was painting it, the pastor informed her. It was inconceivable that her husband was that kind of man. She was a brilliant woman—talented, capable of earning a living for herself and the three children—but there was a time when she did have a financial struggle. Money is an important and realistic issue for children as well as adults. This is especially true when the family's standard of living is substantially lowered quite suddenly. The woman in this instance didn't want to put this added worry on her children. Awareness of the economic realities, however, soon became only too real to the older of the three. Did the church come to her aid? No, and she finally felt it was necessary to remove herself and the children from that scene. Her husband had long since departed, of course, and she had remained at this "church home," hoping against hope that this could at least be one stable force in the lives of herself and the children. Eventually she remarried, but not before she had moved on to reestablish her life successfully, developing remarkable coping skills in the process, rising above the distress of her situation.

How did she do that? "It took a moment by moment reliance on God's help as I moved through the maze of problems," she confesses. "But His grace and help *are* sufficient." In even this she became an overcomer. She never gave up on God; she did have to give up on the man who abused her children, even though the church did not believe her and, in fact, urged her to stay with the marriage. Today, happily remarried, she enjoys the security of a stable marriage, and her children have a wonderful stepfather. Now they all live in peace.

WHO GIVES PEACE?

Peace is possible. Although it may not seem attainable at times, especially in the early days of a divorce, it can and does come. In my own case, I found refuge in Isaiah 26:3: "Thou wilt keep him in perfect peace, whose mind is stayed on thee: because he trusteth in thee" (KJV). That which most often generated feelings of unpeace came from others.

Peace may seem elusive when you are struggling with a decision to remarry or not to remarry. Perhaps you are listening to those who, like "Job's comforters," may mean well, but are causing you a lot of anxiety. On the other hand, it may come from your conscience, and the "still, small voice" may be trying to get through to keep you from making another marital leap that isn't right for you.

A good rule of thumb whenever you have ambivalent feelings about a decision is to wait. Who gives peace? God is not the author of confusion, but of peace (see I Cor. 14:33; while the context there is not talking about divorce and remarriage, it is a transferable principle in our decision-making processes).

Questionnaire respondents indicated one thing in particular that they shared in common; it was a feeling of deep inner peace once they had weathered the initial criticism, the shock of their contemporaries, and accompanying trauma. What we all learned was that God can be taken at His Word. If we will trust ourselves to Him, He will not fail us (see I Pet. 4:19). Sweet peace, as the songwriter says, is "a gift of God's love." For me it came when I stopped living a lie.

I met a brilliant Chinese man in his mid-forties who explained to me the problems in his culture in accepting divorce and remarriage. When he was eight years old, his family fled mainland China as communism was closing in. In Taiwan they sought refuge and, in time, came to the United States. In this country he received his education and married an American girl.

"I should have listened to my inner warning signals; the marriage was not good from the outset. But we did have three children, and we were married fifteen years. During these difficult years, my wife was unfaithful to me and when I discovered that she and a leading elder in our church were having an affair, I sought and obtained a divorce. Our home was strife-filled; there was little if any peace most of the time."

The guilt he felt as a result of this failed marriage and divorce was overwhelming. Then he came across my book, *The Other Side of Divorce*, in the church library. "I can't tell you how it helped me, how it cleared things up for me and gave me inner peace," he said. How well I remember his call—he had gone to some lengths to track me down to thank me for helping put him back together emotionally.

"Now I want to do something for you and for others in China," he had said. "I want to translate your book into Chinese." A year later he sat in my office, a radiant smile on his face.

"I've remarried and my wife is Chinese, too. We waited a long time for her father's consent—he is so opposed to divorce and remarriage, and it relates back to our Chinese culture and heritage. But, finally, my wife's sister and other family members told us to go ahead without her father's consent, and we did. While we long for his approval on our marriage, we know we have God's approval. We are so very happy. I have never experienced such inner peace in my life. I know this is right, contrary to what many in the church say. God gives that kind of peace."

Chapter Eleven

Are You Ready to Be Married Again?

Both divorce and remarriage bring change. I have talked to many people crushed by divorce who confided that they feared the changes. That is certainly normal.

One man told me, "I discovered that my family and friends isolated themselves. I was shocked to find out how unprepared I was for this. I had to go out and make new friends, and it took a long time before some of my own family even came around. I went through all the disappointments and changes that one runs into as a second-class Christian because of divorce; then later it was intensified because of remarriage. In the remarriage we handled it just by being quiet about it, I guess, and little by little the problem ceased to be so formidable, and finally became no problem at all. It was a Mount Everest then."

If it's any consolation, I've told divorced people that even though divorce is a rough experience, and remarriage is full of changes and the unexpected, divorce today is not what it once was in Moldavia. (A principality of what now is a part of Romania.) In the sixteenth century, there were no alimony, no support payments, no separate maintenance, no legal fees, and no court costs. Alexandru Lapuseanu, Moldavia's ruler from 1546 to 1568, simplified matters greatly. He just imposed the death penalty on anybody who even started divorce proceedings.

IS THERE LIFE AFTER DIVORCE?

But there are those who question: Is there life after a divorce? Some of the happiest days of my life were spent in the immediate years following my suicide attempt. I did not realize it nor fully appreciate the change that had come over me at the time, but I finally caught on that here I was single (alone), free to be me, earning a decent salary, and responsible really to no one but myself. Yes, I had children to consider, but they also benefited from the change that had come over me. They were my responsibility, but in freeing myself from the restraints that had so marred my marriage, I was also freeing them from many submerged fears. If I wanted to stay in bed on Saturday morning and catch up on some needed rest, I could do that; if I wanted to go shopping and just wander around the malls, I could go; I could experiment with redoing my home, work at improving my mind through reading and studying, travel, relax—whatever I wanted within the limits of my finances. But I was independent. I was driving the Southern California freeways to and from work, but even that was made pleasurable by listening to good radio programs and salvaging the time in thoughtful meditation. Truly, I had found joy in change and acceptance of the present.

Someone has said that it is seasonal work being single, and you never know how long your season will be. Neither can you direct whether spring will follow winter. You have to just wait and hope and see. There are times when you lead a very exciting life, and other times when you have no company but yourself. There are times when Mr. Right (or Ms. Right) seems to have walked into your life and then just as suddenly he (or she) is gone.

But one day a gentleman did walk into my life, and he's been around now since Valentine's Day in 1974 when we were married. I wasn't looking for anyone; I wasn't contemplating or expecting remarriage. It just happened.

QUESTIONS TO ASK BEFORE MARRYING AGAIN

One of the saddest things counselors hear today is that a man or woman did not look long enough before marrying the second time. In our loneliness, we can be tempted to remarry too soon. The folly of our poor judgment can rise up to haunt us the rest of our lives if we are not careful. I caution individuals to ask themselves some questions before seriously considering remarriage. (These questions are not in any special order of importance—they are all important.)

1. What do I need in a mate?—not just what do I want!

Analyze your own emotional makeup; seek professional guidance if you are uncertain. You may not be qualified to say if this is necessary or that; you may not be objective. Rather than run the risk of repeating your first-time mistakes, seek help. Perhaps such help can come from those who know you best—a close friend, family members. Or, you may need professional help.

One widowed-remarried woman confided that her pastor warned her not to marry a certain man, that from his knowledge of her and her first happy marriage, he felt she was making a mistake. Did she listen? No. Is she sorry today? She is no longer sorry because she and her husband finally have worked through their problems, but she was sorry for many years and often chided herself for failing to take her pastor's counsel to heart. "He really did have my best interests at heart," she explained.

What about the advice of family members and friends? How much should you listen to what your own children may be saying? (Remember, children can be selfish, too; they may feel that their relationship with you is threatened. On the other hand, children can be very discerning; weigh carefully what you are hearing.) My own children breathed a sigh of relief when one man I was seeing no longer came around.

Pat answers to these questions would be just that—pat and not reliable. Your family members and friends may be totally reliable and have your best interests at heart; someone else's family and friends might not be. In my case, I listened to Ed and Thelma Elfstrom, my spiritual mother and father. They were impressed with my fiancé's maturity, dignity, humor, and other attributes that they felt fitted my needs. In fact, they gave us a beautiful home wedding followed by a magnificent reception at a very fine hotel.

Sometimes you can become so attracted to certain traits in a member of the opposite sex that you get carried away, overlooking certain other important areas just because you are, in a sense, swept off your feet by their charm, mannerisms, and chemistry. *Beware. More than one person has told me that what you see is not always what you get.*

"I always get the dregs in the bottom of the cup," one woman sadly complained. "He is charm personified to everyone else, just as he was with me before remarriage. . . ." This woman, representative of those who leaped too soon, told me she has invested many years and tears in someone she finds difficult to respect. "While the marriage is better than my first marriage, and I think he'd say the same thing, I know it's not what it could and should be."

2. Are our chemistries compatible?

Closely aligned with the first question is this total area of chemistry, which includes not just sexual attractiveness, but appearance, taste (or lack of taste), ability to communicate, values. Are these things in line with what you need from the person you hope to spend the rest of your life with in marriage?

My husband always looks great. Rarely have I ever seen him when he didn't look top-notch. I recall that whenever I saw him (before marriage), his shoes were so well shined you could see your reflection in them. But his manner of dress and his mannerisms were impeccable, and they've always been that way. I happen to like that in a man. In addition, we like the same fun things, we communicated easily on a variety of subjects, and we found our values and priorities matched. Of course, there needs to be a judicious mix of approaches when it comes to evaluating these aspects in another person, but as someone has said, "It's important to like what you see when you wake up in the morning." I liked the way my husband looked; apparently he found my looks okay, too. But I know women and men who have compromised a bit in the looks department when they discovered other attributes in this person checked out with their needs. Looks can be, after all, only skin deep, and we mustn't forget it.

3. Are either of you entering into marriage hoping to change the other afterwards?

The biggest mistake we can make in marriage or remarriage is going into the relationship with a hidden agenda—the idea that we will work on changing his (or her) ways after we are married. Everyone I've talked to emphasizes that this is a common and horrible mistake. It is enervating—physically, emotionally, and mentally draining. It produces an unending conflict of wills, and it is ultimately destructive to the relationship.

Bob Brown talks about this in his book *Getting Married Again* where he shows the need for *philos*, friendship, in the man-woman relationship.[1] It's a kind of profound companionship where we are comfortable and accepting of the other. "*Philos* requires an effort at understanding."[2] Brown explains that we have the right to question the behavior or the attitudes of one we love, but such questioning should be designed to gain understanding, never to accumulate data for the next fight or to provide arguments for the next assault in the unending effort to change the one we love. To marry someone with the idea that he or she has potential, seems pliable, and will be easy to control (*manipulate* is really the right word), and that, in time, you'll get them to do those changes you want, is to invite trouble. With understanding, therefore, there must also be acceptance and trust.

4. Is this person a man or woman of integrity?

Trust has to do with integrity. No hidden agendas.

Honesty is an absolute must, so very essential if a relationship is to thrive and grow. Your stakes are so high this time. You don't want to make another marital mistake. Can you believe what this person says? Is he (she) trustworthy? Nothing will destroy a relationship quicker than a breach of trust. Can you really be yourself with this person, or do you have to wear a mask? Does this person admit his limitations and that he's not perfect? Is he constantly defending himself? Can you share your needs, hurts, and hopes? Look for integrity—honesty and stability, uprightness and sincerity—and someone who is a person of principles.

5. Is your mate-to-be a Christian?

I could never have remarried an unbeliever or even someone who was a fence-straddler, a nominal sort of Christian. The Bible says not to be yoked with an unbeliever (see II Cor. 6:14). What about marrying someone from another faith? One woman shared that she married a Catholic and that this has been a heartache in her remarriage. "Many times I have longed to have him there beside me in church," she wistfully stated. He would go his way on Sunday morning; she would go hers. He wanted his children raised Catholic; she wanted hers raised Protestant. Understandably, that situation could create some problems. They did work it out, and they and the children survived, but this woman cautioned against marrying someone whose basic religious beliefs are quite different from yours. Her husband is a believer, but they do not agree about everything.

This woman asked, "If you can't worship and pray together, what do you have in a marriage? Isn't that basic?" At least she and her husband could pray together, which they did, and she felt this was one of the "glues" that helped hold their marriage together.

Wisely, this man and woman had discussed this aspect of their relationship before remarriage. He stated that he had leveled with her on every possible question and issue that might arise in their marriage, "as a marriage with issues held back to be corrected after remarriage will only destroy that marriage." He wanted to be married in the Catholic church, and she agreed to that. Actually, she had wanted both her pastor and the priest to officiate at the ceremony, but her pastor's church board would not allow him to have any part in the ceremony. There was much opposition to their marriage (each had been widowed), and the pressures were especially heavy on the woman. This man showed a great deal of faith, wisdom, and maturity.

"I was very worried at this time and began to wonder if I was doing the right thing. I didn't want a wife who did not love and trust me, and if Ann couldn't be a loving and trusting wife, then she would be better off without me. This worried me a lot, but I had no one to discuss it with. It was not something to burden a friend with, and I couldn't go to the priest or to the minister. I felt that I would just have to let things work themselves out. I used to take long walks during my lunch hour. . . . During these walks I had a lot of time to think and to sort things out in my mind. I used to get in most of my praying during this time. I felt really close to God when I was outdoors like that. During one of my walks, I prayed that God would help me through this problem and in regard to our remarriage. If He didn't think it was right, then He should somehow give me the message. I wanted a sign. As I walked along, I decided that if she would refuse to marry me in the Catholic church, I would consider this a sign not to go ahead with our plans. I knew in my own mind that I would have married her in no church or even in her church as I was really in love with her, *but I wanted to do God's will and not my own.* I knew that I was weak, but I was really willing to back out if that was His sign to do so. I was completely satisfied then and felt like a huge burden had been lifted from my shoulders.

"As it turned out, Ann decided to marry me in the Catholic church, and I thanked God that she had done so. I felt that God had decided in favor of remarriage for the two of us."

It turned out to be an elegant and unusual wedding, with both his and her children participating.

As for Ann, she had done considerable dating after being widowed. She was an attractive woman—petite, charming, exceptionally intelligent, efficient, and poised—but she wrote:

"I had my two children, my home, my church, wonderful friends, and a good part-time job. My first husband had left me financially independent. After some months, when friends insisted that I begin socializing, I accepted a dinner invitation at their home. They'd picked out a wealthy, good-looking single man as my partner for the evening, and two other couples were also invited. They were all very successful, swinging singles, I found out later. I felt terribly out of place, and their language, stories, and everything about the evening offended me.

"But it was the start of getting me out. . . . Finally, however, I gave up on the dating scene and decided that the children and I would do fun things together as we had done before men entered the picture. But then I met Doug at work; we had lunch together a few times, and he invited me out for dinner.

" *'Why, oh why, had I been so foolish to accept his invitation—what was the matter with me—hadn't I definitely decided I wouldn't date again?'* This was the question I asked myself on that Saturday as I realized the time was drawing closer for him to come by for me to keep our dinner date. And, of course, that was the beginning."

She appreciated Doug's openness and honesty. They had long discussions about their children, their religious differences, and what they expected of each other in remarriage. And when Ann's pastor was not allowed to participate in their marriage ceremony, while she was disappointed, she knew this was not sufficient reason to keep her from marrying this good man whom she had come to respect and love.

"He never interfered with my religious beliefs," Ann stated, "nor I with his. At times we've differed in our views, but we've been courteous to each other, not demanding, and we've lived up to what we agreed upon and decided about this aspect of remarriage before we married."

6. Do you share interests?

I'm an avid reader; I love to write. My husband has enjoyed a successful musical career. How awful it would have been if he didn't enjoy sharing my love of books and discussing them, or if he hadn't approved of my writing. How equally distressing to him it would have been if I had no music appreciation. What are your likes and dislikes? How do you mesh in these interests?

7. Has this person realized his or her aspirations?

By this I mean is this person a fulfilled person? Have any of his or her dreams come true? Or is he or she frustrated, insecure, and basically a dissatisfied, unhappy person even though he or she does a good job of covering up? Does he or she have goals for the future defined? What are his or her priorities?

8. Finances.

This is a touchy subject. You'd better cover it before remarriage. Will he be expected to support you and your children? Remember, child support monies don't always come through. Have you discussed this possibility with your mate-to-be? Do you think women should *expect* to be supported? After all, if you're single and divorced, you've no doubt been supporting yourself; most divorced women do. Many of today's couples who are marrying and entering into remarriages don't consider that it is essential for the man to support the woman. Each woman's needs and expectations are different, but I understand there are men who say they won't marry a woman who doesn't work and bring in her share.

Can he support his children by a former marriage? Does he have spousal support payments to make? In these times, women also have to make both kinds of payments, although spousal is rarer. (In a previous chapter I told you about Mitzi, who is making child support payments. If Mitzi remarries, I hope she will be wise enough to talk this over with her husband-to-be before she marries him; this situation could present problems otherwise.)

My husband made monthly alimony payments for ten years—right up until the time his first wife died. At times that was a struggle and a sacrifice, but we never missed payments and willingly increased them through the years. These are practical realities that you must face before remarriage when you are marrying someone who must make spousal support and/or child support payments.

The most beautiful and heartwarming story I've heard as it relates to finances was shared by a couple I'll call Gail and Tom. Tom's wife left him for another man, taking their two daughters with her. Gail's husband died of cancer, leaving her with five children. Both Gail and Tom were in their mid-forties when they met. Remarriage for them has not been without its areas of conflict, but they resolved them with intelligence and compassion.

Shortly after their remarriage, Tom's first wife learned she had terminal cancer. Her new husband, who didn't want to be saddled with a woman who was going to die of cancer, walked off—taking the television, the car, and leaving her and her daughters high and dry. Destitute, she appealed to Tom. Gail and Tom had her and her daughters moved from another state back to the community where they lived. Because she was unable to work, they provided for her every need. She actually lived longer than the doctors estimated she could survive. This was, understandably, a terrible financial drain on Gail and Tom. Gail never complained and pitched in, using much of the money she'd been left by her deceased husband, to help out. In the end, they lost their home.

I think the thing that stands out the most in my own thinking is what Gail did for this dying woman, her husband's first wife. She visited her in the hospital and assured her she'd never try to take this woman's place with her daughters, but that she would care for them and give them a mother's love. Because the dying woman had lost all her hair, she was wearing wigs, and Gail took it upon herself to clean and set the wigs, helping this woman to maintain her appearance as best as she could right until the moment she died. She also insisted that Tom be with his first wife and the daughters as much as possible, and that he be there at her bedside when she died.

Could you have done that in a similar situation?

Financial compatibility is a definite plus. You can have very distorted and unrealistic attitudes toward money that can create some dynamite problems in remarriage. Those I've talked to or who responded to the questionnaire admitted that this was one of the most difficult adjustments they were forced to make.

If you are a man who wants a career-oriented woman, don't pick someone who longs more than anything else to stay at home and raise children, dogs, and cats. If you like assertive women, an ambitious professional person, then you are headed for trouble if the woman you fall for doesn't meet those expectations. On the other hand, if you are attracted to the stay-at-home type, but the woman you are seeing is career-minded, then your longings will not be met here either. What do you want from a wife? Define your expectations before taking that second-time-around plunge.

One man said:

"Money and the children's welfare combined to become a high priority problem that we faced in remarriage. There were times when I felt I couldn't handle it another day. It is something that should be talked about before you commit yourself to a new marriage. The problems won't just go away because you choose to ignore them; and, in fact, they are liable to tip over on you as something greater than you can handle after remarriage. I suggest a good, clear-cut understanding before you enter into a relationship at all.

"As a matter of fact, I think every one of these practical aspects of a remarriage relationship involves principles that should be discussed between a man and a woman who are looking forward to remarrying. The problems are out there—they are many-dimensioned—and you can't just hide away from them or hope they will go away after remarriage. I might add you can't even pray your way around them. *There are certain things you have to do.* We have to be doers of God's Word, and if we are not willing to do what He wants us to do as it relates to remarriage, then we are better off to stay out of the marriage altogether."

Money is almost always a problem after divorce and remarriage. Divorce often destroys your economic security and necessitates a change in your standard of living. Are you prepared for that? Do you have or need a prenuptial contract? What is yours? What is his or hers? Have you made out your wills? These are considerations, especially when you both have children.

In our case, my husband had two married sons; I had two

married children and two unmarried and living at home at the time of the remarriage. We made out a prenuptial contract and our wills. I had certain family heirlooms that I wanted to make certain were passed on to my children. Furthermore, I had worked hard to refurnish my home, and I wanted to make certain my children would receive some of those things if anything happened to me. Selfish, you say? Not at all, as far as I'm concerned. When you've worked as hard as I've worked—disciplined yourself, applied the seat of your anatomy to the seat of your chair and faced the typewriter and the wall for years on end (yes, literally years), you don't want to have it all go down the drain. Your children deserve to share in what you've done and acquired; after all, they had to give up their mother's time and attention while she worked, so they deserve to reap some of the goodies. I also had the prospect of some book royalties accruing in the years ahead which I wanted to protect for my son's education. (As it happened, I wasn't writing pornography or gothic novels, so we didn't do so well in the royalty department.) Nevertheless, these are practical areas of remarriage that confronted up front can save yourselves and your children much heartache later on.

One woman told me this has been an area of conflict in her remarriage—she and her husband didn't draw up a prenuptial contract and wills; now she can't get her husband to agree to anything, and they aren't getting any younger. "He's already had open heart surgery, and this is a concern to me. I regret that we didn't face this head on at the time we talked of remarriage. If that love is real, if he's not marrying you for what you've got, or vice versa (she marrying him), it shouldn't be an area of conflict."

9. Have you dealt with the "formerlies"?

Are you certain you can deal with the past in your remarriage? (How will you feel if he calls you by his first wife's name?) Do you have a clear picture of what went wrong in your first marriage? Have you pieced together a sound picture of your potential partner's former marriage as well as given her the insights necessary so she can do that as well? Remember, rarely are there good guys and bad guys. Don't kid yourself;

you undoubtedly contributed *something* to the failure of that first marriage. Get rid of your self-righteousness. Nobody is perfect. Try to be objective and honest. One writer suggests you listen carefully to your intuition. When you are on the verge of marrying again, you may experience some strong hunches: you may feel comfortable moving toward remarriage, that this is the way to go. On the other hand, you may experience some very ambivalent feelings. Stop and think: "Is the Holy Spirit trying to tell me something?"

Another area of "formerlies" relates to the memories each of you have gathered through the years. Sometimes the presence of those memories and recollections can throw one or the other of you off balance. They can also induce a certain amount of sadness. My husband likes to recall a trip to Europe that was so memorable. I wasn't a part of that. At first it hurt, but now I've become accustomed to it, and I realize that this was really a significant event in his life. Why shouldn't he talk about it at appropriate times? I'm equally certain when he hears the children and me recall our happy Christmases, that he experiences a twinge or two. There's a certain fragmentation that goes along with a second marriage that is inevitable, a disconnectedness, if you will, a discontinuity, and it's just there. The mind just doesn't discard impressions formed through the years of a former marriage, and this again is especially true when there are children involved. If you are not careful, these remnants of a former marriage, or of the time when you were divorced and living as a single, can intrude and jeopardize a remarriage. The stress imposed can lead to jealousy and sensitive, hurt feelings. Some jealous feelings are normal and really only show that you or the person you love care enough to have such a reaction. But it can be inappropriate and troublesome when you needlessly aggravate it in each other. To be irrationally possessive or needlessly provocative will only drive a wedge between you and your spouse.

10. How does this person you are contemplating remarrying hold up under stress?

Be honest at this point. Remarriage is going to put a real strain on your relationship. Can it take it? At this point, listen to family and friends whose judgment you trust. They may be able to give you valuable insights you aren't willing to face. Is this really a quality relationship?

One woman told me that the most disillusioning aspect of her remarriage is the fact that her husband can't take stress, that the moment something goes wrong at work he threatens to quit—that this has put a real strain on her living under that kind of uncertainty. Furthermore, she related that he takes out his frustrations on her and the children—she understands that a person has got to be able to let off steam and unwind, but this has been a very difficult aspect of remarriage that she wasn't prepared for.

Remember too, if you have children in the home, that this person is going to be their stepparent. If there is any one thing that came through from the questionnaires, it was this solemn fact. The biggest problem each encountered had to do with stepparenting. This is STRESS in capital letters.

11. Is the relationship between this person you are contemplating marrying and the children (yours and his/hers) a good one?

If it isn't all that either of you would like it to be, and you observe this before remarriage, then stop, step back, and analyze it as carefully as you can. There are many excellent books on the subject of stepparenting. You should read up on the subject before tying the knot. One book in particular that I like is by Dave and Bonnie Juroe, dear friends, entitled *Successful Stepparenting: Loving and Understanding Stepchildren.*[3]

Well over half of all divorces involve couples who have children. In the 1980s well over a million new children each year are experiencing the breakup of their parents' marriages. Actually, about one in every six children in this country is a stepchild. What that indicates is a lot of tender hearts that have been broken. It's a traumatic social phenomenon that must be acknowledged, and churchgoing people are not exempt. The major area of conflict in my marriage has been over my children—possibly because two of them were still in the home at the time of remarriage. This has brought stress into our relationship, causing a lot of heartache, and I still have one unmarried college-age son.

Others have shared that their children are living longer at home, due to the economy. Some couples have said they couldn't afford the tuition and college expenses, so the college-age kids are still at home—attending local colleges and working part-time. It's tough—just plain tough—when your kids get older, are doing more thinking on their own and want to express their opinions, when they are struggling with financial problems, when they sense the stress. The problems and tensions have been much deeper than we anticipated. Let's face it—blood runs thicker than water. The natural parent is going to be somewhat defensive for whatever reason. It is not my intent to belabor the subject of stepparenting in this book. I do, instead, urge that you read the beforementioned book and others that the Juroes recommend. However, I do want to emphasize and caution you to go into a remarriage with your eyes wide open when there are children involved.

The woman I mentioned earlier (who married the Catholic man with six children), was very frank about their problems. All told, between the two of them, they had eight children to handle. She said, "You will do your readers no favor if you don't tell them the truth about stepparenting. Today our children are all grown—many of them married, others still struggling their way through college, and we have a strong, loving bond as a blended family. But it takes time and patient persistence. I couldn't have done it without the Lord's help." She relates how after their honeymoon she came down to the kitchen in a lovely, frilly bathrobe to fix breakfast for everyone. The children had all beat her downstairs, and they were already at it—squabbling amongst themselves, fixing breakfast, and sacks of school lunch.

"There sat my husband his face buried in the paper, oblivious to it all. . . . Of course he was accustomed to this, but I wasn't. Besides, I was a new bride. I just flew back up the stairs, flopped down across the bed and cried!"

She looks back on all of it now ith good humor, but at the time it spelled stress.

12. Are you certain you have allowed enough time between your divorce and remarriage?

A number of respondents indicated that they probably should have waited longer, or that they at least should have gone together longer. I believe women make this mistake more often than men; on the other hand, a man whose wife has left him might marry on the rebound to restore his damaged ego.

Sometimes people allow themselves to be propelled blindly into another marriage without having resolved the reasons for the failure of the first marriage. There may be a subconscious desire to seek revenge on the partner in the first marriage. Pride enters in—loneliness and anxiety—will I ever find someone else? I'd better jump at this chance while the getting is good. A desire to reestablish a way of life that was lost through divorce leads people into second-time-around marital mistakes. Poor judgment enters in.

The more insightful you can become about reasons for the failure of your past marriage, the better are your options for happiness in remarriage. To do this takes time; it also requires that you test yourself in new relationships and that you do some comparing and contrasting. Don't be in too much of a hurry to remarry. Allow yourself time to change.

Frederic F. Flach, M.D., writing in *A New Marriage, A New Life*, has these words of wisdom: "If you wait a few years after a former marriage has ended before marrying again, you will usually improve your chances of choosing well. You will have had that much more time to learn about yourself and understand your relationships with others, and you will be more likely to be governed by common sense than by wishful thinking."[4]

Notes

1. Bob W. Brown, *Getting Married Again* (Waco, Tex.: Word Books, 1979).
2. Ibid., p. 129.
3. David J. Juroe and Bonnie B. Juroe, *Successful Step-Parenting* (Old Tappan, N.J.: Revell, 1983). Dave and Bonnie have a blended, reconstructed family that includes eight children—five of them are Dave's by a previous marriage, two of them are Bonnie's, and a third is "theirs." In the appendix of their book, they give additional suggested reading recommendations for success in stepparenting.
4. Frederic F. Flach, M.D., *A New Marriage, A New Life* (New York: McGraw-Hill, 1978) p. 82.

Chapter Twelve

Remarriage Is . . .

Remarriage is, one man wrote, among other things, taking once again the risk of failure. "But," he added, "the effort is clearly worth it. In fact, in a funny way, the effort *is* it—the very act of trying, of working to be less rigid, giving up our most irritating habits, altering our most destructive attitudes—this is the source of our intimacy and of our growing self-knowledge. We are becoming each other's best, and most sympathetic, critics."

We live in no bed of roses. Our marriage, with stepchildren and money problems and all the other difficulties that typically accompany second marriages, is full of tension. But I've learned that I never again want to be with a woman who's not as strong as I am. I've also learned that I need a wife, that being married is part of my identity. . . . The great, slow dance that is marriage remains the best way for the vast majority of us to balance our masculinity with its opposite, to give point to our sense of responsibility and, finally, to bear the sometimes overwhelming burdens of this life.[1]

. . . A TIME FOR LEARNING

Hope springs eternal in the human heart, but without large doses of common sense, it can easily become myopic optimism. Second marriages bring with them complex problems. There are many pitfalls, unreal expectations, and a much more complicated set of human relationships than you encountered in your first marriage. High on your list of needed personal assets must be courage. Add to that love, flexibility, creativity, and coping skills, along with a strong religious faith, and a mutual desire to make this marriage work—not to expect perfection, but to sincerely learn from past mistakes, and make the most of this new opportunity. Then, you are well on your way to marital happiness the second time around.

I am well aware that the twelve areas discussed in the previous chapter, with related questions to ask yourself, are a lot to expect to find in a remarriage partner. You may be thinking that if you meet someone who lives up to even half of those things, you'll be doing good.

Barbara Johnson, author-friend whose optimism is a constant source of encouragement to me (and, I might add, to thousands of others), gave me this image, which someone had given her: a bad marriage is like trying to hold a beach ball under water twenty-four hours a day. Someone else has said it is like trying to hold a dozen pingpong balls under water—they keep bouncing back up, first one problem area here, then another there. Just about the time you think you've licked one problem and handled one difficult area pretty well, something happens in another area. Is there an ideal marriage anywhere, a perfect man and woman sharing blissfully all that a marriage relationship has to offer?

One writer on marriage tells of seeing a bumper sticker that said, "Stamp out first marriages." Someone else said, "Everybody should be married once to prepare themselves for marriage." Still another individual remarked, "The whole experience of being married and then being single again gives you a greater insight into who you are. In my second marriage, I am very clear about what I need and want out of life."

A happily remarried woman responded to my question of "What do you think of such statements?" (as the ones above) by writing:

"We don't prepare ourselves adequately and properly the first time in marriage. I can't think of anything we enter into (with the exception of parenthood perhaps) more ill-prepared than we do in marriage. At least with parenthood you have a lot of books and nine months to read them and prepare for the coming child. We don't do this in marriage; at least I didn't. I know that today many pastors won't marry someone until they counsel them at a few premarriage sessions, and there are good books out on the subject of preparing yourself for marriage. I think, however, that the people who read such books are probably in the minority (judging from the divorce rate in this country). Also, if a couple make up their mind to get married, I seriously doubt very many of them would give it up if the pastor counseled them against it.

"But as for remarriage, I cleared it up in my head as to what I needed, and what was right for me. *I also knew what I didn't need.* I think in many respects I always knew what I needed, I just didn't get it the first time around because I didn't approach it properly.

"In answer to your question, 'Is there an ideal marriage . . . a perfect man and woman sharing blissfully . . .?', my remarriage is more than I ever dreamed a marriage could be. If I go back to my childhood and think about what I thought a marriage was going to be, then this marriage is all of that and more. Truly, I am absolutely thrilled, and it is working. This marriage is ten times more work than my first marriage was, and praise the Lord, we care enough to work at it."

I asked questionnaire respondents how they felt about the words from the song, "Love is lovelier the second time around," and what about the sexual relationship in remarriage—is it what they had expected and hoped for?

"Well, love is there the second time around, at least in my case," one woman stated candidly. "I never knew it was possible to love someone the way I love Steve, and our sexual relationship is but an expression of that love. It's exciting because I had come to the conclusion in my first marriage that sex was not a very nice part of life. Now I enjoy everything about our relationship so much that it enhances the sexual relationship. For me it is definitely lovelier the second time around."

Many others responded in similar ways—that true love was missing in the first marriage, that there was too much selfishness or lack of respect one for the other, that kept the relationship from ever developing its full potential.

Jan D. said she felt that Mike, her second husband, is the only man she's ever been married to. "If it weren't for my daughter by my first marriage, I wouldn't really say I'd been married before. That first marriage seems like a bad dream, and I've forgotten most of it. When I remarried, I understood men better than I did the first time around, so in the second marriage I was able to sort out my needs from my wants, knowing myself better too, and I was much more careful about whom I dated. I really weighed my options carefully, taking many things into consideration. As a result, remarriage is all I expected it to be *and much more.*

"Our sex life is great because Mike is my first love. I think lack of communication in a marriage starts in the living room and is carried to the bedroom. Because we have so few communication problems, our sex life is just that much better."

The former pastor turned counselor mentioned in chapter 4 admitted that he chose to remarry partly out of pride.

"I was so crushed by the weight of the divorce—remember, my first wife divorced me—that when I suddenly realized that everything had gotten out of control, I felt somewhat less than a man, I guess, and I rushed into a second marriage. I know that my second wife sensed that this was a possibility because she asked me if I was sure I wasn't still carrying a torch, or if I was marrying on the bounce. I denied it vehemently, but I am afraid the truth of the matter is that I just wanted to show the world that I was still marriage material. But there are deeper and better reasons for remarriage, of course. Now when people come to me about marriage, I insist that they work out a dozen or more potential problem areas beforehand. When it comes to counseling for remarriage, I try to help the individuals realize how their first marriages broke down, how I let these problem areas get away from me, and how we can take these same problems into a second marriage.

"My own second marriage was bound to explode in another divorce, and just by the grace of God, and in the nick of time, I realized what was going on and began to take responsibility for my actions. It was a civil war all over again until I realized that the basic responsibility for the well-being of the home is the husband's responsibility. He is to be the head of the house; God has made him responsible. If things go wrong within the home, it should be laid right at his door, and he has to understand that he is responsible. To the degree that he can be made to realize this, to that degree there is the possibility of preventing divorce. Of course it requires the wife's cooperation, but I must admit that Jesus who showed perfect love for the world was rejected, and so a simple man, trying to show Christ's love to his wife, has no guarantee that she will accept it, so there is more to it than appears on the surface. But I put the monkey on the husband's back, and I did this to myself. Even though there are always two sides to every marriage, and I agree that basically no one person is totally responsible for the failure of a marriage, I insist that the primary responsibility for happiness in a marriage or remarriage, belongs to the husband. And I am telling it as I see it and as I experienced it. I tell people, 'Hey, you are just asking for another set of troubles, and unless you are prepared for them, you had better not go into remarriage.'

"I am constantly reminding myself that it is better to prevent a problem than to try to find the answer to a problem. Of course a problem-free life is an unrealistic goal, but the more you eliminate before you get into a remarriage, the less severe they are going to be."

The woman whose husband had died and then who married a man whom she later discovered to be an alcoholic, and divorced him, emphasized the need to be cautious about marrying again. "Make up a list of the characteristics, a value judgment of what you want and need in another husband (or wife). Certainly in a second marriage, one should have learned much from prior mistakes, and bring more wisdom to the marriage. Remember, as we grow older, we do become more inflexible, so this needs to be taken into consideration. Some people may be so set in their ways that they cannot or will not change, and so the mistakes they made in their first marriage may get carried right into a new relationship, and you may inherit a whole new set of problems that you didn't have in your first marriage. They may be much worse than the first marriage."

Someone said that divorce is a catalyst causing people to change themselves. Sometimes this can happen only with the aid of counselors and psychiatrists. But we *can* gain a new self-awareness and get in touch with our feelings, thereby approaching remarriage with a more clear picture about what we want out of life.

One man said that with his first marriage, "We just staggered along with constant put-downs, temper tantrums, and spoiled and immature attitudes," but that in his second marriage, both he and his wife are happy, excited, and at peace with themselves and God. "I wake up every morning wondering what new miracle is going to take place today. The big difference in this marriage is that we read the Bible and pray together, we have fun—no longer do I go around looking like I've been baptized in vinegar—when we do have things that bug us, we get it out in the open and talk about it intelligently rather than fussing, fuming, and fighting. We are real with each other. We are authentic. Above all, we are open to God's will. I am deeply in love with my wife; she is an incredible gift from God."

An articulate woman wrote: "Remarriage is wonderful when it's God-directed, but it's not easy. As a Christian, I have a stake in the marriages of fellow believers—in their joys and sorrows—when I have it within my understanding and knowledge to help them. So many people are hurting, disillusioned, and ready to give up; tell them divorce isn't the best way, but if it's happened, it's not the end of life. As a remarried woman, I have a common bond with my ex because of our children, but sometimes the old wounds do surface, and they will for that person who remarries. *But Jesus heals.* We may get tossed around, fearful even, but with Jesus at the controls of the boat, the storm won't destroy us."

Respondents seemed to indicate that a contented sex life

and sexual fidelity are much more likely in the second marriage. "We are very affectionate and playful," one woman said. "There is really no comparison, as far as I'm concerned, to my first marriage."

Another person, a man, said, "Ours is such an intimate relationship—difficult to explain, but wonderful. It's much more sexual than either of us had before, on that we are agreed, but it's also a more intellectually stimulating relationship, and I think that is bound somehow to the physical relationship. There's a total commitment to each other, which results in contentment and a deeply satisfying happiness."

Leslie Aldridge Westoff, writing in *The Second Time Around: Remarriage in America*, has delved into the reasons for what many call "super sex" in remarriage. "The men and women I interviewed were unanimously positive about the importance of sex in their new lives. Sex the second time around was a devastatingly delightful experience, an incomparably thrilling emotion, a revitalization of all the senses that make life so pleasurable."[2] She refers to documented fertility studies that show both men and women having sex more often in their second marriages (regardless of age and of the duration of the second marriage—some of which were longer than the first marriages).

Westoff explains that part of the reason for sexual success in a remarriage may be that the couple wants love, sex, and a new secure life acutely at a time in their lives when they have been out of the mainstream. They want back in badly, and they are very receptive to sex with love. Also, those who have been through marriage before are more sexually skilled, more mature, and more aware of themselves and their partners, and what will bring sexual satisfaction. "After some years of marriage," a woman admitted, "the sex starts going downhill. And to be able to start it again . . . the hunger and appetite of youth, with the experience of years of practice, can be unbearably exciting. Not more exciting in the sense that it is new. But more exciting in the sense that it is more unexpected, more varied."[3]

Couples revealed that second marriage partners seemed less inhibited, that there is a greater sexual naturalness; a candidness and honesty in every aspect of the relationship; a heightened degree of communication; a pride in each other's accomplishments; a greater tolerance; a sharing of interests; an appreciation of each other's attempts to be funny, wanting to make each other laugh; less feeling fatigued and bored with life; more understanding, sympathy, and empathy. Westoff says, "This heightened awareness, this internal radar that is constantly awake and scanning, means not only that couples are familiar with what it takes to make their marriage work, but that they actually try harder to make the marriage succeed."[4]

Everyone I talked to told me that remarriage for them meant working harder to make it work, that they felt they made better choices the second time because of their awareness of how necessary it was not to fail again and that this paid off when problems did appear (as they do). Couples told me they tried to avoid arguments and that petty things that made them upset in their first marriages were not a problem in the second. They weren't as selfish; they were more willing to see their partner's point of view.

. . . A PHENOMENON WHOSE TIME HAS COME

Second marriages are flourishing. Remarriage is a phenomenon whose time has come. Let's face it; remarriage is the major alternative to remaining divorced and single for Christians whose moral standards are such that they cannot be sexually promiscuous—and this is the biblical admonition.

Usually it is best to be married, each man having his own wife, and each woman having her own husband, because otherwise you might fall back into sin. . . . I'm not saying you *must* marry; but you certainly *may* if you wish. I wish everyone could get along without marrying, just as I do. But we are not all the same. God gives some the gift of a husband or wife, and others he gives the gift of being able to stay happily unmarried. So I say to those who aren't married, and to widows—better to stay unmarried if you can, just as I am. But if you can't control yourselves, go ahead and marry. It is better to marry than to burn with lust. (I Cor. 7:2, 6-9 TLB)

These are the Apostle Paul's words. Of course, he wrote them to unmarried individuals, or to those who were no longer married because they were widows or widowers. But the *truth* of what Paul said applies to divorced people as well. Truth is truth, regardless to whom it was spoken.

If unmarried people fall into sin because of their sexual needs, and if they find it difficult to maintain control, and they "burn with lust," the same thoughts, feelings, and emotions are experienced by divorced people. So the same *truths* apply.

Paul understood the involvements in marriage because the Holy Spirit was directing him in what to write, but also it is commonly believed that he was either a widower or a divorced man himself. There are those who believe Paul was from a well-to-do family, and that after he became a Christian, his family disowned him. That may have included a wife. He was also a member of the Sanhedrin, and most believe a man had to be married to attain that position. Yet Paul said he wished everyone could get along without marrying, just as he did (I Cor. 7:6). The point is *he was unmarried at that time*. Why didn't Paul say he was a widower or divorced? Why is there no historical record not only of his marriage, but of his children (if he had them)? What Paul did say about himself is that he was the worst of sinners (see I Tim. 1:15). He went on to say "But for that very reason I was shown mercy so that in me, the worst of sinners, Christ Jesus might display his unlimited patience as an example for those who would believe on him and receive eternal life" (v. 16 NIV).

Why did Paul feel he was chief among sinners? That is certainly the way we divorced people have felt, isn't it? And too often, when we remarry we are made to feel that way by inflexible, legalistic Christians. Perhaps Paul said nothing about his past because, when sin is confessed, God not only forgives but forgets it. Although Paul acknowledged that he had been the chiefest of sinners, he reminded his readers that he and they were new creations in Christ Jesus. This truth is too often overlooked or conveniently ignored. We need to remember that when divorce is confessed as sin, God's forgiveness comes with his forgetfulness of that sin. In the eyes of our merciful Lord, the one who is divorced is not a divorcee but single. Hebrews 8:12 tells us that when God forgives wickedness, He remembers our sins no more (see also Heb. 10:17).

One theologian wrote me that from personal observation and experience, as well as from what the Bible teaches, he would say that the most important attributes for two people in a marriage are *love* and *forgiveness.* "This can only abound as you know the fullness of God's love for you, and of His tremendous forgiveness for you, and then to realize that that same magnitude of love He has for you, and that same forgiveness He has for you, is for your spouse too. The Lord takes these sins in our lives, and as we repent of them, learn from them, and grow in Him, He gives us new opportunities by our love, compassion, understanding, and care to manifest in our lives what He has accomplished in us. So before remarriage, ask yourself if you have enough love for that person you are contemplating marrying, and if he or she has children, do you have enough love for an extended family, and do you see enough of Christ's love in that person? One cannot have the character or the integrity that is needed unless one is right with Christ."

Another theologian stated: "We enter into a triangle, a covenant relationship between a man and a woman, where God is at the pinnacle, and His Word is the foundation of this triangle. To me that is the only way marriage, at any level, is going to work out, and even then it is not going to be a perfect relationship, because at least two of the people in the triangle relationship are sinners—sinners saved by grace, but still subject to making all kinds of mistakes because we are also still human. Once that is understood, and the couple covenant together to do everything within their power, and by God's grace and help, to play out their role as nearly perfectly as possible, then there exists the possibility that they will have a glorious husband-wife relationship."

A PLACE FOR GOD TO WORK

In conclusion, I would like to quote from a book on the complex issues involved in marriage, love, and sexuality by Ray

S. Anderson, Associate Dean at Fuller Theological Seminary, and Dennis B. Guernsey. I am especially grateful to Dr. Anderson and Dennis Guernsey for the loan of this material while it was still in unpublished form. Dr. Anderson points to the rising divorce rates in recent years, calling it a *dis-ease* in the state of marriage, a symptom of a more fundamental confusion of human sexuality, linked with a basic incompetence in developing and sustaining mature covenant relationships. In summary, Dr. Anderson states:

> Because God joins himself to the temporal social relationship consummated as a marriage and recognized by society and the church, that marriage is indissoluble on any grounds whatsoever other than the command of God. If a marriage comes to the point of utter breakdown so that it is a disorder, rather than an order of human relationship, and inherently destructive to the persons involved, one can only seek to bring that relationship under the judgment of God. For Christians, this means that the breakdown of a marriage to the point of utter failure is a betrayal of the covenant love that God has invested in that marriage, and is therefore a sin. To attempt to find legal or moral grounds on which to be excused from the marriage contract is, in our opinion, untenable. The scriptural teaching on marriage and divorce clearly brings the marriage under the judgment of God as the one who has the absolute right of determining its status.
>
> If Christians, and the church, do not have a process to deal with sin and grace as a work of God, then there will be little hope for those who become victims and casualties of hopeless marriages. But where the work of God is understood as his contemporary presence and power under the authority of Scripture to release those who are in bondage and create a new status where "all things are new," then the church as the community of Christ will have the courage to say NO to a continued state of disorder and YES to the forgiveness and grace of God, which brings persons under a new authority of divine healing and hope. We are speaking here, by analogy, of a "death and resurrection" experience as the work of God in the midst of human lives. To create a "law of marriage" that would deny God the authority and power to put a marriage to death and to raise the persons to new life through repentance and forgiveness, would appear to be a desperate and dangerous course of action. What God has joined together, indeed, let not man put asunder. But where God puts asunder as a judgment against sin and disorder, and therefore as his work, let not man uphold a law against God.
>
> It would be misleading to end this essay on marriage as the expression of love and sexuality on a negative note. The command of God by which

marriage as a human, social relation is given the status of covenant partnership is a positive and rich resource of growth and renewal. What God "joins together" he attends with love and faithfulness. This is a promise and commitment of God himself to the marriage relation as a source of love, healing, and hope. The Christian community participates in this work of God by providing a context of support and enabling grace for each marriage that belongs to the community.

Those who undertake the calling of ministry to families through pastoral care and counseling have as their first priority the ministry of encouragement and support for marriages. This ministry is a constructive and positive reinforcement of marriage and prevents the deterioration of marriage into a shell of the love and commitment it is meant to express. God is faithful to weak and problem-plagued marriages—not merely angry at unfaithfulness.

God is patient and loving to marriages where love has been lost—not merely angry at our own anger and lovelessness. God is hopeful toward marriages which are ready to crash—not merely angry at our incompetence. God never gives up on his "joining together" because God himself is the covenant partner of marriage. This produces a bonding that never is allowed to become bondage.[5]

I come to the end of this book—an undertaking that has stretched out over four years—with a certain reluctance, yet a sense of satisfaction. Yes, now it is finally completed, this writing that has been the most difficult I've ever attempted and that has taken me the longest to do. There is always a certain ache in my heart, a sadness, if you will, that I had to be a marriage casualty. From the time I was a little girl, I have wanted to please God. I have also tried, with His help, to please others, not disappoint people. So the writing of this has been difficult. I have wanted so much to bring healing and help to those hurt and traumatized, as well as stigmatized by divorce. I have wanted the chapters to help the church better understand the complexities of divorce, the loneliness that results, the feelings of guilt, the sadness—all that accompanies the breakup of a marriage. I have wanted to remind us that God Himself said it was not good for us to be alone. God's desire for our fulfillment, coupled with His forgiveness, forgetfulness of past sin or failure, marvelous mercy and grace, means that divorced individuals need the help of other Christians as they seek to get on with living (*and* with loving again), if indeed another person comes into their lives.

My plea to the church is simply this: Give the divorced and divorced-remarried Christians in your midst another opportunity. By the grace of God, exhibit His mercy, forgiveness, understanding, and love. Be walking love to the walking wounded.

Healing Prayer

> At every moment of our existence,
>   You are present to us,
> Father,
>   in gentle compassion.
> Help us to be present
>   to one another,
> so that our presence
>   may be a strength
> that heals the wounds of time
>   and gives hope
> that is for *all* persons
>   through Jesus, our Lord and merciful
> Savior.
> (Author of this revised poem-prayer unknown)

(I urge the reader to be sure and read the appendix, which follows. I have included some very important observations there, contrasting the two most prevalent opinions among Christians today regarding divorce and remarriage, and I believe you will find this material of great significance.)

Notes

1. Anthony Brandt, "What Divorced Men Are Looking For," *McCall's* (May 1984), p. 16

2. Leslie Aldridge Westoff, *The Second Time Around: Remarriage in America* (New York: Penguin Books, 1977), p. 126.

3. Ibid., p. 129.

4. Ibid., p. 140.

5. Ray S. Anderson and Dennis B. Guernsey, *On Being Family: Essays on a Social Theology of Family*, from chapter by Ray S. Anderson entitled "Marriage as an Expression of Love and Sexuality" (Grand Rapids: Williams B. Eerdmans, 1985).

Appendixes

Appendix I

Statistics

Statistics are not totally reliable, but the availability of men and women according to the "Never Married," "Widowed," and "Divorced" categories, based on U.S. Census Department figures for 1983, are shown below:

WHO'S AVAILABLE?

AGE	NEVER MARRIED		WIDOWED		DIVORCED	
	MEN	WOMEN	MEN	WOMEN	MEN	WOMEN
20-29	11,503,000	8,512,000	21,000	69,000	764,000	1,287,000
30-34	1,804,000	1,230,000	3,000	69,000	798,000	1,042,000
35-44	1,214,000	929,000	45,000	308,000	1,298,000	1,911,000
45-54	638,000	517,000	148,000	718,000	881,000	1,221,000
55-64	430,000	970,000	323,000	2,077,000	527,000	857,000
65-74	390,000	458,000	622,000	3,542,000	254,000	467,000
TOTAL	15,979,000	12,616,000	1,162,000	6,783,000	4,522,000	6,785,000

Based on U.S. Census Department figures for 1983

Other vital statistics facts show that there are only twenty-six million unmarried men for thirty-four million unmarried women over age eighteen. Looking at it as a game of musical chairs, that means eight million women don't have a place to sit down when the music stops.

Who is likeliest to remarry? Men are. Approximately 62 percent of divorced men remarry within five years, compared to 54 percent of women. According to sociologist Andrew Hacker, "The younger a divorced woman, the better her chances of remarrying."

Who marries whom? Close to 56 percent of all marriages in 1984 were of two never-married people; 22.7 percent were of two divorced people; 9.8 percent involved a divorced woman and a never-married man.

How successful are second marriages? The divorce rate for second marriages is higher—at 57 percent—than for first marriages. Why? Some say it's because people don't find out why the first marriage failed, and they continue to make the same mistakes. They blame their partners for all their marital problems instead of dealing with their own failures. Andrew Cherlin of Johns Hopkins University adds that few couples are prepared to cope with the unique complexities of a second marriage—stepchildren and former in-laws, for example. And Frank Furstenberg, of the University of Pennsylvania, contends that people who have already been divorced are less commited to remaining in an unhappy marriage than those who are still in their first.[1]

I have always found statistics to be highly manipulable, subject to interpretive measures by those wanting them to serve their particular bias. When it comes to statistics on divorce and remarriage, most people have a definite opinion, one way or the other. Furthermore, today's statistics will be outdated tomorrow. However, a book such as this generally includes some statistical information, thus this appendix.

To my knowledge, there are no reliable statistical records showing how the divorce and remarriage ratios among Christians compare to the overall divorce and remarriage statistics nationwide. We would like to think that there are fewer divorces in the church. Judging from the growing number of singles groups and conferences for singles, and from talking to a number of pastors, and my own observations in the cities we have lived in and the churches where we have worshiped, I believe that divorce among Christians is widespread and growing. However, there is an encouraging note to all of this—for most churches today do recognize the problem, and many of them have taken a compassionate stance, providing a special ministry to them. Others, unfortunately, while recognizing the problem, still insist that the consequences of sin do not automatically disappear and brand the divorced and remarried so they cannot serve or participate in certain aspects of the total church ministry. The attitude of these churches has been explained in *Meant to Last*, an excerpt of which follows:

Across our nation courageous pastors . . . are refusing to encourage divorce or to marry previously divorced persons.

A recent Gallup poll for *Christianity Today* revealed that a surprising percentage of Americans still believe divorce should be avoided under all circumstances and that remarriage after divorce is acceptable only in cases where the former mate is dead. The survey covered the full spectrum of denominations, both liberal and conservative theological persuasions. It showed that evangelical clergy, persons who have had a conversion experience, those who are frequent Bible readers and frequent churchgoers take a more conservative view than others. For example: 27 percent of frequent Bible readers believe that remarriage following divorce is never permitted and 25 percent of Baptists (other than Southern Baptists) do not believe divorce is ever justified.[2]

Reading those statistics another way, one could say that 73 percent of frequent Bible readers believe that remarriage following divorce is permitted, and that 75 percent of Baptists (other than Southern Baptists) believe divorce is justified. So you see what I mean about statistics being highly manipulable and subject to interpretive measures.

The writers of the book from which I have been quoting, ask the question: What is the place of the divorced person in the church? and quote some more statistics and make statements like this:

Remember that marriage is an illustration of the relationship between Christ and the church (Eph. 5:22-33). Divorce spoils the illustration and defaces the picture. Once a divorce has taken place, perhaps followed by remarriage to another partner, the typology is marred. It is not surprising then that limitations are placed on the divorced person when it comes to service in the local church. To ignore the fact of divorce would be to ignore the priority God has placed on the permanence of marriage and the high qualifications the Bible sets for church leaders.

The 1982 General Conference of the Evangelical Free Church adopted a policy forbidding the licensing or ordination of those who are divorced or married to one who has been divorced.

We contacted ninety mission boards serving the foreign field. Over one-half would not consider divorced people for career missionaries; over one-third would not accept divorced candidates for short-term service; and nearly 20 percent would not even consider divorced people for home staff (secretaries, accountants, etc.). Most of the missions responding indicated that under ordinary circumstances, divorce is a serious disqualifying factor to a missionary candidate.[3]

In contrast to the statement in the book, *Meant to Last*, is the observation by Bob Brown in *Getting Married Again* that the church accommodates other difficult teachings of Jesus, but that "we have, as churchmen, literally interpreted and enforced the ideals of Jesus regarding divorce and remarriage. We have universally disregarded some of the New Testament teachings and have said they cannot be applied literally in our world. Yet we have persistently said that the divorce and remarriage ideals can be applied literally."[4] That is an observation made in one way or another by many other writers and theologians—many of whom I have quoted in this book, others whom I have listed in the Suggested Reading section following this appendix.

Brown points to Jesus' Sermon on the Mount—much of which we are unable to interpret literally and act upon absolutely. Dwight Hervey Small points to this also, pointing out that the first three Synoptic Gospels—Matthew, Mark, and Luke—link the New Testament with the Old Testament. "They form an historical transition in which many dominating concerns are Old Testament concerns. That which has come must relate to that which was prophesied," according to Small, "and this is the burden of the Synoptic Gospels and the Book of Acts. This is not the burden of John's Gospel or the Epistles. The Synoptic Gospels form that important bridge."[5] "The Sermon on the Mount has an eschatological setting, that its first, primary applications are sometimes to the future Kingdom," Small points out (see p. 46, *The Right to Remarry*). We are living in the Church Age, the age of grace, an ethical interim between the ministry of Jesus during the period of His life on earth when the chief burden of His early ministry was the offer of the Kingdom to Israel, and His second coming to

187

establish His Kingdom reign. "An observation which most writers on the subject of divorce and remarriage seem to miss is that the recorded words of Jesus are found in the midst of His teachings concerning the Kingdom," says Small (p. 44). "The Kingdom has not been seen as that which is to be consummated in the future" (p. 46).

So what does this have to do with the Sermon on the Mount? Simply this, we do not throw out these beautiful teachings, of course, anymore than we throw out anything else in the Word of God, but let us look at some of those teachings (to do this, you will need to get your Bible):

> **Matthew 5:33:38**—Most of us do, at one time or another, take oaths as a witness. Sometimes our laws require this.
> **Matthew 5:40-42**—The church does not judge or excommunicate the person who refuses to grant a loan or who refuses to give a coat to anyone who asks.
> **Matthew 5:29-30**—I've never seen a fellow Christian tear out his eye, and throw it away; nor have I seen anyone cut off his right hand because it's making him stumble.
> **Matthew 6:6**—How many Christians do you know who pray in closets?
> **Matthew 6:16**—Is fasting a traditional religious exercise for you personally, or in your church?
> **Matthew 6:19-21**—Do you have any IRAs? or a savings account? or other investments (treasures)?
> **Matthew 5:27-28**—Do you think you are totally innocent of adultery? Look again at what Jesus said.
> **Matthew 5:21-22**—Does your church advocate murder when one of its members has something against another member?

What do you do with these teachings? These are God's righteous ideals. Would you agree with that? Could Jesus have been laying before His hearers (and us) that which will be characteristic of future Kingdom rule—when He comes back again to reign as King with His bride, the church? Because we don't do all these things in the here and now, does that place us under His condemnation? Should it place us under judgment? Should it put us under the judgment of the Church?

Yet, we take Jesus' words, spoken to Pharisees who were trying to trick Him up, testing Him, regarding divorce and remarriage, and we say this is as it *must* be for Christians. Hear what Dwight Hervey Small has to say about this—his argument is persuasive:

If the Church chooses to feel embarrassment over the conduct of its members [because of divorce and remarriage], let it choose more likely targets—the inveterate gossips, the proud and pompous officeholders, the affluent who do not share their wealth with God's needy ones. Divorced persons have borne the office of the scapegoat long enough. The new embarrassment is that the Church cannot minister to the divorced in her midst because her theology of divorce and remarriage has been found wanting. . . . There is indeed an uneasy conscience in the Church today. Is not the God of grace and compassion speaking? Have we ears to hear and hearts to respond? Or are we relieved that there is a group of God's people on whom the accumulated guilts of the Church can rest? Where else in all the sphere of human relationships may the healing, redemptive ministry of the Church be better displayed than among those whose intimate life has suffered dissolution?[6]

Yes, where else, indeed! The point is, if the church is going to be literal, then it should at least be consistent and not single out divorced and remarried people.

Notes

1. Susan Dundon, "Who Makes the Best Second Husband?" Woman's Day, September 11, 1984, pp. 52, 59.
2. Paul E. Steele and Charles C. Ryrie, *Meant to Last* (Wheaton, Ill.: Scripture Press, 1983), pp. 143, 144.
3. Ibid., pp. 146, 147.
4. Bob W. Brown, *Getting Married Again*, p. 26.
5. Dwight Hervey Small, *The Right to Remarry*, p. 47.
6. Ibid., pp. 177, 178.

Appendix II

Suggested Reading Material

Many books have been published in recent years on the subject of divorce and remarriage. It is not my intent to list them all; rather, I have chosen to select only a small number of them that I believe will minister to those who are hurting or seeking help—books that will not add to your guilt and pain. (Some of these books may be out of print, but you may still be able to find them in a church library.)

Anderson, Ray S. and Dennis B. Guernsey. *On Being Family: Essays On a Social Theology of Family*, in particular the chapter entitled "Marriage as an Expression of Love and Sexuality." Grand Rapids: William B. Eerdmans, 1985.

Brown, Bob W. *Getting Married Again*. Waco, Tex.: Word Books, 1979.

Ellisen, Stanley A. *Divorce and Remarriage in the Church*. Grand Rapids: Zondervan Publishing House, 1980.

Galloway, Dale. *Dream a New Dream*. Wheaton, Ill.: Tyndale House, 1975; *How to Feel Like a Somebody Again*. Eugene, Oreg.: Harvest House, 1978.

Hosier, Helen Kooiman. *The Other Side of Divorce*. Nashville: Abingdon Press, 1975.

Hurst, Gloria. *No Valley Too Deep*. Chicago: Moody Press, 1978.

Krebs, Richard. *Alone Again*. Minneapolis: Augsburg Publishing House, 1978.

Lovett, C. S. *The Compassionate Side of Divorce*. Baldwin Park, Calif.: Personal Christianity, 1975.

McRoberts, Darline. *Second Marriage*. Minneapolis: Augsburg Publishing House, 1978.

Rambo, Lewis R., *The Divorcing Christian*. Nashville: Abingdon Press, 1983.

Richards, Larry. *Remarriage: A Healing Gift from God*. Waco, Tex.: Word Books, 1981.

Ripple, Paula. *The Pain and the Possibility*. Notre Dame: Ave Maria Press, 1978.

Roberts, Patti, with Sherry Andrews. *Ashes to Gold*. Waco, Tex.: Word Books, 1983.

Small, Dwight Hervey. *The Right to Remarry*. Old Tappan, N.J.: Revell, 1975.

Smith, Harold Ivan. *Single Life in a Double Bed*. Eugene, Ore.: Harvest House, 1979; *One-Parent Families*. Kansas City, Mo.: Beacon Hill Press, 1980; *Tear-Catchers*. Nashville: Abingdon Press, 1984.

Smoke, Jim. *Growing Through Divorce*. Eugene, Ore.: Harvest House, 1976.

Towner, Jason. *Jason Loves Jane, But They Got a Divorce*. Nashville: Impact Books, 1978.

The following books are those that I have found to be quite inflexible in regard to divorce and remarriage if the parties involved do not have one of the commonly accepted biblical reasons to divorce and remarry. I list them because I want the reader to be aware. Also, in all fairness, this presents the other side of the divorce-remarriage controversy.

Adams, Jay E. *Marriage, Divorce, and Remarriage in the Bible*. Phillipsburg, N.J.: Presbyterian & Reformed Publishing Co., 1980.

Duty, Guy. *Divorce and Remarriage*. Minneapolis: Bethany Fellowship, 1970.

Laney, J. Carl. *The Divorce Myth*. Minneapolis: Bethany Fellowship, 1981.

Steele, Paul E. and Charles C. Ryrie. *Meant to Last*. Wheaton, Ill.: Scripture Press, 1983.

Recommended books on the subject of stepparenting, by no means all-inclusive of this subject matter:

Hart, Archibald D. *Children and Divorce*. Waco, Tex.: Word Books, 1982.

Juroe, David J. and Bonnie B. *Successful Stepparenting*. Old Tappan, N.J.: Revell, 1983.

Roosevelt, Ruth and Jeannette Lofas. *Living in Step*. New York: McGraw-Hill, 1976.

Other recommended reading material on the subject of divorce and remarriage (not written from a Christian viewpoint) may provide help and guidelines as you seek to rebuild your life:

Flach, Frederic. *A New Marriage, A New Life*. New York: McGraw-Hill, 1978.

Hunt, Morton and Bernice. *The Divorce Experience*. New York: McGraw-Hill, 1977.

Hyatt, Dr. I. Ralph. *Before You Love Again*. New York: McGraw-Hill, 1977.

Krantzler, Mel. *Creative Divorce*. New York: M. Evans and Co., 1973; *Learning to Love Again*. New York: Thomas Y. Crowell Co., 1977.

Reingold, Carmel Berman. *How to Be Happy If You Marry Again*. New York: Harper & Row, 1976.

Westoff, Leslie Aldridge. *The Second Time Around: Remarriage in America*. New York: Penguin Books, 1977.

I wish it were possible to share with you the *many* books that have helped me and influenced my thinking. I do recommend that you become familiar, if you aren't already, with your local Christian bookstore. I would hope, too, that your church has a library. Competent bookstore people and librarians should be able to point you in the direction of books and resource materials that will enrich your life.